Tolerant Oppression:

Why promoting tolerance undermines our quest for equality and what we should do instead

Dr. Scott Hampton

First published by Dog Ear Publishing
4010 W. 86th Street, Ste H
Indianapolis, IN 46268
www.dogearpublishing.net

ISBN: 978-160844-627-8

This book is printed on acid-free paper.

Printed in the United States of America

What is tolerance?

1. A sophisticated hiding place for disapproval, anger and hatred
2. A subtle expression of a condescending attitude
3. An ineffective conflict resolution strategy
4. A natural successor to segregation
5. The shadow of intolerance
6. Never the best option
7. Widely promoted
8. All of the above

Tolerant oppression

All forms of oppression (e.g., sexism, racism, homophobia and many others) are characterized by unequal status and power between groups and the abusive exploitation of that power by the dominant group. Prevention and intervention efforts that fail to address the underlying inequality are doomed to failure. For example, the "separate-but-equal" doctrine did nothing to improve race relations; anger management classes for batterers have endangered adult victims and their children; and the promotion of tolerance has coincided with a dramatic *increase* (not decrease) in active hate groups. Collectively, these strategies that narrowly focus on the cessation of violence, without addressing the underlying entitlement and privilege that endorse that violence can result in "tolerant oppression." (*"I am not allowed to attack you, but I will continue to look down upon you with disapproval and seek more subtle forms of control and domination."*) It is time for us to move past the era of tolerance. This book will help to illuminate the path.

Table of contents

List of exercises

Introduction

"The history of the past is but one long struggle upward to equality."

Elizabeth Cady Stanton
American writer and women's rights activist

In 2003, I went to Washington, D.C. to participate in a sexual violence prevention training put on by a wonderful organization, *Men Can Stop Rape*. During the training, one of the participants told me about a relatively new initiative designed to combat hatred, prejudice and discrimination. Spearheaded by prominent civil rights leaders, the project offered powerful educational materials accessible through a well-designed website. It seemed like a tremendously valuable resource.

What caught my attention when I saw the materials was the focal point of the campaign – the promotion of tolerance. On the surface, that made a lot of sense. Since intolerance is the poison of hate groups, I quickly reasoned that tolerance must be the antidote. Still, the term bothered me. Why? To me, tolerance carries with it an air of condescension. *I don't like you, but I guess I'll just have to tolerate you.*

Why make tolerance the focal point of an international campaign? Why not choose a more positive term, such as acceptance or respect? Surely there are plenty of better alternatives?

When I returned home from the training, I started to do some research. How do other people view tolerance? Have others voiced similar concerns? This book is the fruit of my inquiry. I have found commentaries from religious and civic leaders cautioning us against promoting tolerance. Lay people expressed confusion. Members of oppressed groups said that they were offended by the concept. Members of supremacist organizations claimed that being forced to tolerate those they despised was the justification for their attacks. Tolerance causes problems for everyone.

So why was there simultaneously passionate support and vehement objections to the very same movement? How could allies in the promotion of civil rights and religious freedom be so far apart on this one issue? Was there a way to understand those differences in order to reunite behind a shared vision of eliminating hatred and embracing equality?

To begin to answer those questions, I spoke with people whose organizations promoted tolerance, and those that did not. In addition, I conducted a small study within my nonviolence education classes to elicit people's reactions to tolerance. The purpose of this book is to share with you what I learned.

The study on tolerance

In 2004, 111 members of nonviolence classes were given a questionnaire asking them to compare tolerance with five other concepts (respect, appreciation, understanding, acceptance and trust). Respondents included 98 men (86 Caucasian, eight African American, and four Hispanic) and 13 women (12 Caucasian and one Hispanic). The age range was 18 to 66 with a mean age of 35. The questionnaire consisted of 47 multiple choice items, including 34 interpersonal situations (e.g., *"John would like to invite Bill over for Thanksgiving dinner." "John hates Bill." "John wishes Bill would just go away."*). Respondents were asked to select which attitude was most consistent with the situation in question. For example, if John wanted to ask Bill over for Thanksgiving dinner, would John most likely respect, appreciate, tolerate, understand, accept or trust John? The questionnaire also included 13 personal value items (e.g., *"What would you most like to get from an intimate partner?" "What would you most like to get from a best friend?" "What would you most like to get from your children?"*). If they could receive only one from each of these people which they most want? Would they want to be respected, appreciated, tolerated, understood, accepted or trusted? They also were asked to predict which concept would most likely (and which would least likely) make the world a great place to live. Finally, the respondents were invited to share comments and reactions to the questionnaire in general and to the concepts in particular. Many of their reactions to the promotion of tolerance are quoted anonymously throughout this book.

The importance of equality

The shared vision or ideal of equality (i.e., equal opportunity, regard, protection and rights) forms the basis of this discussion. Without equality, when one group of people believes that it is superior to or more deserving than another, terrible things begin to happen (e.g., religious wars are waged, Hitler seduces his followers to exterminate Jews, Whites feel entitled to enslave Blacks, adults exploit the elderly and children, employers refuse to hire people with documented disabilities, men rape women, heterosexuals pass laws "defending" marriage against homosexuals and pimps prostitute women and children).

So the question addressed here is: Does tolerance support or undermine our efforts to achieve equality? Is it part of the problem of hatred and discrimination or part of the solution? I believe that the promotion of tolerance is a significant part of the problem. We can do without it – much better, in fact.

Why then has the promotion of tolerance gained such traction? Part of the answer is the rationale for its promotion. Reasons I have often heard include: *"We promote tolerance because it is the opposite of intolerance." "Tolerance is just another word for acceptance." "Tolerance might not be perfect, but it is a first step." "You can never end hatred, so in some cases, tolerance is the best you can hope for." "Being tolerant says a lot about someone's character."* These perceptions are important to address and will be covered throughout this book.

Another part of the answer (as to why tolerance has become so popular) might be found in our nation's history, during the post Civil War period. As a nation, we struggled to the realization that one group of people was not entitled to own or enslave another. While the institution of slavery was outlawed, the supremacist attitude that fueled it remained.

Welcome segregation. *If I can't own you, at least I can banish you.* But even then, there was a concern about equality (e.g., equal access to basic life necessities). So the doctrine of "separate but equal" was born. You can justify excluding people from your school, train car, theater, etc. as long as you offer so-called equivalent services for them elsewhere. We thought that separate actually could be equal. I imagine that there could have been segregation campaigns analogous to the tolerance campaigns of today, with slogans like *"Fight slavery, promote segregation."* Trusted leaders such as President Lincoln and influential authors such as Harriet Beecher Stowe were behind the movement. Few challenged its wisdom and were so bold as to suggest that "separate" undermined equality. As we look back on it today, the problems of segregation seem obvious. (*If we all are truly equal, why would we need to be separated?*) We can follow a similar path with tolerance or we can recognize tolerance as a new hiding place for hatred, just as segregation once was, only this time more subtle and sophisticated.

In our search for equality, we are in a time of great hope. In the U.S. we recently came close to putting the first woman on the presidential ballot, while we elected our first African American president, one who is committed to promoting inclusiveness. (Perhaps this contributed to his being awarded the 2009 Nobel Peace Prize.) We are also in a time of great concern. According to the Southern Poverty Law Center, there has been a steady rise in the number of active hate groups in the United States, from 602 in the year 2000 to 926 in 2008, a 54% increase in less than a decade! While slavery was outlawed over a century ago, in practice it still exists, even in this country, in the form of human trafficking. While de jure segregation has been forbidden for decades, de facto segregation continues to thrive. According to researchers from the Civil Rights Project at UCLA and Harvard University, segregation was worse in some urban areas in 2000 than in the 1970's.

While we have made progress, we are still doing some things terribly wrong. For example, attitudes such as "tolerance" tell us how to act *when we hate*. Not good enough. We need to shift our focus onto *how not to hate*. Only then can we approach equality and peaceful co-existence in any meaningful way.

Tolerant oppression

To explain what I have learned about tolerance, I use the term "tolerant oppression," and suggest that this view of tolerance has three components: (1) *Inequality:* Similar to other oppressors, tolerant oppressors believe that the person or group of people being tolerated is inferior, less deserving, flawed or evil. (2) *Entitlement:* They feel entitled to control, dominate, exclude or otherwise oppress the objects of their tolerance. (3) *Restraint:* Unlike other oppressors, the tolerant ones feel temporarily restrained from acting on the desire to control their targets. This restraint is due to their belief that they are being forced to "put up with" people of whom they disapprove, distrust, perhaps even hate.

It is important to note that not all tolerant people are oppressors. For example, human trafficking victims might feel compelled to tolerate their circumstances until a rescue or escape can be arranged. They are not oppressors. Quite the opposite, they are the oppressed. Tolerant oppression becomes more likely when it is the people in power who are tolerant. As Mark Twain once said, *"Whenever you find yourself on the side of the majority, it is time to pause and reflect."* He understood the dangers of unequal power.

Some people in the dominant culture actively and deliberately abuse their power as a way of dominating and controlling others. Their oppressive thoughts and actions might be the most obvious. But even those with good intentions are not immune to thoughts or actions that are experienced as oppressive by others. For example, consider a parent who is cooking dinner with a young child. The child is struggling to open a bag of frozen peas with a pair of scissors. Noticing the child's frustration, the parent steps in and says, *"Give me the bag. I can do it more quickly."* The child protests by saying *"But I want to do it."* The parent overrides the child's wishes. *"No, it is taking too long. You can try again next time."* Was this an act of oppression, or an attempt to rescue the child from the discomfort of frustration or just a wise time-management decision? How would the child feel? What if the parent took over repeatedly, each time the child attempted to learn a new skill, explaining how it would just be more efficient if the parent did it? Would that be oppressive? What would be the impact on the child's sense of competence and self-worth? Do you think the parent's goal was to oppress the child? Everyday examples like this suggest that we all must be mindful and vigilant about how we use our power and influence. Oppression is not exclusively the province of hostile hate groups.

There are people who promote tolerance who have no desire to be oppressive. In addition to tolerance they advocate for acceptance, respect, appreciation, understanding, inclusiveness and other positive concepts. They might be unaware that even the well-intended promotion of tolerance undermines their otherwise socially beneficial programs. My hope is that the stories and perspectives reported in these pages will encourage them to move beyond tolerance to less ambiguous and more compassionate and hopeful approaches.

Another distinction to keep in mind as we evaluate tolerance is the difference between tolerating *what people do* and being tolerant of *who they are*. If their behavior is hurtful (e.g., they are physically attacking you), group membership is not important. You should not have to tolerate the attack and there is nothing oppressive about your insistence that they stop their violence. But if your disapproval is based solely on their racial, religious, or other group membership, then your attempts to change them, make them leave or otherwise comply with your demands are more likely to be oppressive. If you decide that you just have to put up with them for a while, we might refer to that as tolerant oppression (i.e., your disapproval is present and active, even though your *overt* attempts to control them have been temporarily suspended).

Those who thrive on telling other people what to do or how they should live are often aware of this distinction. They know that if they speak out directly against who people are, they will be accused of being racist, homophobic, sexist, etc. To appear less judgmental, they seek to identify and demonize behaviors that other groups engage in so that they can appear to be taking the moral high ground (e.g., they might say that they are *"seeking only to protect our way of life"* even when their way of life is not actually being attacked). We will examine how the dominant culture engages in this form of oppression in several areas of our lives (e.g., drug laws, prostitution and pornography, sports, marriage access, domestic violence, sexual expression).

How to use this book

As I was preparing to write this book, I was amazed at the wide range of reactions I heard about a proposed book on tolerance. *"Of course tolerance is useless. Do you really think you need to write an entire book just to say that?"* *"Wow, I never thought about it in that way [that tolerance is condescending]. It makes perfect sense."* *"A discussion like this is long overdue."* *"Don't you think it's just a matter of semantics? What difference does it make what word you use?"*

This diversity of reaction was matched only by the diversity of backgrounds of the people whose thoughts are shared in this book. You will read about the views of religious leaders from many Christian denominations, Judaism, Islam, Buddhism, Hinduism and others. You will also find comments from civic leaders, educators and lay people. Perhaps most compelling for me were the reactions from members of oppressed groups, those who have been targets of hatred or discrimination based on their sex, race, religion, sexual orientation, age, ability, class or country of origin. As it turns out, they are not big fans of tolerance.

The structure of this book was chosen to offer flexibility to the reader. While you can read from start to finish, you also can skip around, without worrying about whether a previous chapter or section of a chapter provided a necessary foundation for the current one. You could even use it in a "page-a-day reflection" format if you want to spend extra time with a particular thought.

To get the most from the material, you might want to use it as a workbook either by yourself or in discussion with classmates, colleagues, family or friends. I have included 30 exercises from my workshops and classes that are designed to help us examine our assumptions, feelings and reactions. Through these exercises, you will have the opportunity not just to read what others have said, but to practice what they have learned. These are exercises that have been posed to civil rights and gender studies classes, in batterer intervention programs, during domestic and sexual violence trainings and at legislative hearings. The goal of these exercises is to provoke thought and discussion rather than to figure out the "correct" answer. The first exercise, presented at the end of the introduction, is good preparation for reading the rest of this book and contains questions to keep in mind as you read about other people's experience with tolerance.

Topical content

The beginning of this book exposes tolerance as a subtle or sophisticated form of oppression by addressing the relationship between tolerance and related problems such as intolerance and hatred. Later chapters contrast tolerance with alternative concepts (e.g., equality, acceptance, respect, appreciation, and understanding).

The impact of "tolerant" attitudes on many topics and issues is discussed throughout, including domestic and sexual violence, homophobia, human trafficking, corporal punishment, terrorism, discrimination against those with documented disabilities, suicide, abortion, chemical dependency, racial profiling, conflict resolution, managing grief and others. As you will see, the effects of promoting tolerance and the values underlying it are far-reaching, encompassing our personal health, interpersonal relationships, community welfare, and even international struggles.

Exercise 1: What is your personal experience with tolerance?

Purpose: To identify your own starting point with tolerance in preparation for examining other views.

Think of a time when you felt the need to tolerate a person or group of people. Was the need to be tolerant due to who they were or what they were doing? If it was what they were doing, was the behavior directed toward you? Was it causing you harm or inconvenience? How did you feel? Were you annoyed, angry, fearful, or disappointed with them? Or were you happy, excited or pleased with them? When you noticed yourself being tolerant, did you enjoy that experience or were you looking forward to the opportunity not to have to be tolerant anymore? Did your tolerance solve any problem or make any problem worse? Did tolerating other people improve your relationship with them, make your relationship any worse or have no impact?

What about a time when someone told you that you were the person to be tolerated? Has anyone ever told you that they were willing to be tolerant of your lifestyle, your race, your religion? How did or would that make you feel? Would you appreciate their generosity, be insulted or have some other reaction? If you have never been the person who needed to be tolerated, do you feel fortunate, or do you feel left out and envious?

Once you've had a chance to examine your own beliefs, we will begin our exploration of other perspectives with a brief discussion of the views of two of the most respected champions of equality and peaceful co-existence: Mahandas K. ("Mahatma") Gandhi and Dr. Martin Luther King, Jr.

I.

Mahatma Gandhi and Dr. King on Tolerance

Why did neither Mahatma Gandhi nor Dr. Martin Luther King, Jr. promote tolerance as the solution to hatred and intolerance? What can we learn from their decision?

1.

Arun Gandhi speaks out against tolerance

Mahatma Gandhi's Grandson (Arun Gandhi) warns us of the dangers of promoting tolerance. *"In recent decades we have emphasized the value of teaching people "tolerance." Tolerance is not only inadequate, it is a negative concept which only alienates society further. Learning to tolerate absolves people of the responsibility of learning to understand different people, accept and appreciate their differences, and progress towards respecting them for who and what they are. It is only when we build acceptance between people that we will rid ourselves of the scourge of prejudice and liberate ourselves from violence."* Arun Gandhi in "Legacy of Love: My education in the path of nonviolence."

Mr. Gandhi points out how tolerance is inconsistent with (rather than synonymous with) understanding, respect, appreciation and acceptance.

2.

Hitler and Gandhi on tolerance

> *"Make the lie big, make it simple, keep saying it,*
> *and eventually they will believe it."*
>
> Hitler

Repeat the statement that tolerance is good and as Hitler suggested, with enough repetition they will come to believe it.

> *"An error does not become truth by reason of multiplied propagation,*
> *nor does truth become error because nobody sees it."*
>
> Gandhi

On the other hand, as Gandhi pointed out, stating something repeatedly is not enough to make it true; it is just enough to make it dangerous. Hitler persistently spread the notion that Jews were a threat and should be feared. While his repetition of anti-Semitic beliefs did not make those beliefs true, it did generate enough power to fuel Hitler's genocidal attack with catastrophic results.

Tolerance does not cease to be a condescending attitude just because it is widely promoted. Its promotion only makes it more dangerous. This is important to note in light of the fact that, according to the Southern Poverty Law Center, materials to teach tolerance are sent to more than 400,000 educators each year in the United States alone! We should heed Mark Twain's words when he advised us to "[not] *let schooling interfere with your education.*" It is time for us to reconsider what we are teaching our children.

> *"A good decision is based on knowledge and not on numbers."*
>
> Plato

3.

Nonphysical violence

"Any attempt to impose your will on another is an act of violence."

M.K. Gandhi

When we speak of violence, we are usually referring to physical activities such as hitting, kicking, stabbing or shooting. Gandhi viewed violence from a broader perspective to include not just physical but also nonphysical attacks that serve to dominate or oppress people.

While acts of intolerance include the obvious physical attacks, tolerance usually is more subtly expressed in nonphysical ways so that visible scars are rare. Instead, the impact of tolerance is more likely to be emotional, psychological, social or economic. Fueled by condescending attitudes, tolerance suggests that one group considers itself to be superior to and more deserving than another. Gandhi applied this view to religion by suggesting that *"tolerance implies a gratuitous assumption of the inferiority of other faiths to one's own."* Perhaps this statement clarifies why tolerance was not among the values Gandhi actively promoted.

4.

Is tolerance part of Dr. King's "Beloved Community?"

"Our lives begin to end the day we become silent
about things that matter."

MLK, Jr.

Imagine if by some miracle, Dr. King, Jr. were able to return today to a meeting amongst civil rights leaders who were discussing the promotion of tolerance. As he walks into the room, one of them says *"We have good news for you Dr. King. Your efforts at creating the Beloved Community were not in vain. We white people have learned to tolerate your race. Aren't you pleased?"* What do you suppose his reaction would be?

5.

Why Dr. King never promoted tolerance

"Cowardice asks the question, 'Is it safe?' Expediency asks the question, 'Is it politic?' But conscience asks the question, 'Is it right?' And there comes a time when one must take a position that is neither safe, nor politic, nor popular, but because conscience tells one it is right."

MLK, Jr.

Martin Luther King, Jr. never promoted tolerance as a solution to hatred (or to any other social ill he addressed). A review of the collection of his papers at Stanford University found no instances of his promoting tolerance in either his speeches or sermons. If Dr. King never needed to promote tolerance, why do we think we need to? Is it that we think he was not smart enough to consider the benefits of tolerance? Hardly. Is it that he did not have a broad enough vocabulary? Ridiculous. Did he not have time to get around to it? No. He was a prolific writer. Surely, if he valued tolerance, he would have actively and frequently promoted it. Is it that tolerance was too new a term? No. That concept (e.g., as in "religious tolerance") was in vogue as far back as the Roman Empire 2000 years ago. It is more likely that tolerance, consciously and strategically, was simply not part of his vision. Perhaps we should follow his lead.

Certainly there will be resistance to our speaking out against tolerance. There is always resistance to change, but as Dr. King pointed out in the quotation above, we must not remain silent simply because it is safe or politic to do so. We voice our objections to alienating attitudes such as tolerance because it is the right thing to do.

6.

The King Center's Pledge of non-violence

In honor of Dr. Martin Luther King, Jr., the King Center, in Atlanta, GA created a pledge of non-violence asking all who would sign to help make *"the world a place where equality and justice, freedom and peace will flourish."* Their pledge cites many great values that are part of creating the nonviolent, Beloved Community that Dr. King envisioned. Those values include: justice, equality, freedom, peace, unconditional love, courage, compassion and dedication. But in their commitment to *"reject all forms of hatred, bigotry and prejudice,"* tolerance is not mentioned even once. Apparently, they did not believe that tolerance was part of the solution that Dr. King had in mind.

7.

I have a dream . . . that does not include tolerance

"My dream is that one day my children will grow up in a country in which they will not be judged by the color of their skin, but by the content of their character." When directed to a group of people, tolerance always involves judgment, in fact, prejudgment. It does not seek to understand someone's character. Without knowing anything about them as individual people, it assumes their character to be flawed.

Despite Dr. King's choice not to promote tolerance, our persistent promotion of it causes us to misremember history. For example, the "Education World" website had a section called "Tolerance Lesson Plans." In it I found an alleged reference to Dr. King's dream. *"Martin Luther King, Jr., dreamed of a world more tolerant than the one he lived in. This week's lessons are designed to teach kids about King's dream of tolerance."* Dream of tolerance? I can find no mention of tolerance in Dr. King's "I-have-a-dream" speech. Can you? Did Dr. King say *"I have a dream that someday my children will grow up in a country in which white kids will tolerate them?"* Not even close. Hard to imagine he ever would have thought or said that. The more we promote "tolerance," the more we delude ourselves into believing it is a positive concept and the more we believe that some of the great peace keepers in our history also promoted it, when in fact they did not.

As one of our study participants commented about tolerance: *"That's hardly what Dr. King had in mind."*

8.

Popular is not the same as good

"Remember, everything that Hitler did in Germany was legal."

MLK, Jr.

This observation of Dr. King's might help to explain why Hitler was able to garner such power before he was confronted. We often ask *"Is it legal?" "Is it normal?"* or *"Is it common?"* as we decide to reject or accept some policy or perspective. For example, it used to be legal in the United States for men to rape their wives, as evidenced by the marital rape exemption laws that were still in full force and effect in some states as recently as the 1990's. But being legal did not make it any less barbaric or repugnant.

Also in the United States, there was a time when slavery was both legal and popular. Then it was segregation that was both legal and popular. We deluded ourselves into believing that separate actually could be equal. Nearly 60 years passed before the U.S. Supreme Court updated its thinking and deemed that separate was inherently unequal (at least in the educational arena).

Dr. King had a rare ability to step outside of conventional wisdom to detect injustice and inequality. We need to develop that ability in ourselves so that we can take an objective look at tolerance to see how inherently unequal and destructive it can be. Perhaps then we will insist on promoting true acceptance and equality rather than spend enormous time and energy defending such a flawed and hostile concept.

II.

The power of words

From racial slurs to eulogies, words can infuriate or provide comfort. They can galvanize an audience, inspire greatness or incite a riot. They can change history or the course of an election, break up a marriage or be woven together to form a love sonnet. In any event, their power and impact should not be underestimated.

What images come to mind when we hear: (1) Civil rights leaders tell us that we are to practice *tolerance* toward those who are different from us? (2) Sarah Palin, during the 2008 Vice Presidential debate, claim that we live in a *tolerant* society? (3) Supremacists complain that they are forced to *tolerate* people they despise? Do these three statements evoke similar images since they all involve forms of the word "tolerance?" Do we all interpret the messages in the same way? Can we say for sure what the speaker meant in each case?

In this chapter we will examine the importance of language. The words we choose reflect our underlying beliefs; those beliefs determine how we interact with the world. As you will see, the problem with promoting tolerance is not just one of semantics; it has real world and lasting consequences.

9.

The language of hate

Hate groups practice tolerance regularly (until they can't take it anymore and lash out with acts of intolerance). You can confirm this by listening to their language:

"How long should we have to put up with women on the job?"
"Why do we have to let Blacks into our neighborhood?"
"We can't tolerate gays in the military if we want to keep this country safe."

How can you motivate people to change by asking them to do more of what they consider to be the problem?

10.

"We must not forget the power of words!"

These words were spoken by a Simon Wiesenthal Center tour guide. While on a tour of that highly educational facility in Los Angeles, particularly impressive due to its coverage of the Holocaust, I asked one of the tour guides about the promotion of tolerance. In response, this woman (who had relatives killed in the Holocaust) said:

"Of course tolerance is awful,
but I'm afraid that that is the best we can hope for."

I cannot overstate the extreme sadness I felt when I heard that prediction. It was hearing views such as that one that motivated me to write this book. I refuse to believe that tolerance is the best we can hope for. And let us not forget the message, that for good or (in this case) for ill, the power of words should not be underestimated.

Exercise 2: Biased language

Purpose: To practice discovering values and beliefs, hidden in our language, that influence how we perceive and interact with others.

First, identify the misleading implication of the following statements or phrases. Then rewrite each phrase so that the misleading implication is removed. Pay particular attention to the words in bold type. For example, "Tom and Beth are in an abusive **relationship**." *The misleading word is "relationship," implying that it is the relationship that is abusive, rather than one person abusing the other. You cannot tell by the phrase which person is the abuser and which is being abused. By calling the relationship abusive, we are implying that the victim is at least partially responsible for the abuse. A better phrasing would be (assuming that Tom is the one who is abusive) "Tom has been abusive towards Beth by calling her a bitch, physically restraining her, and punching her on* *two occasions." Now you know who is perpetrating the abuse and what the abusive behavior is.*

*War casualties **decreased** this week. (Hint: By the end of last week the total was 1549.)*

*The child rape victim **lost** her **innocence**.*

*He was **not guilty** of murder by reason of insanity.*

*The average age in that group to first engage in **consensual** sex was 12.41.*

*A film with that much violence is for **mature** audiences only.*

*He is a **disabled** veteran.*

*The **opposite** sex*

*He's not **straight**, he's **queer**.*

***Fighting** for peace*

Illegal aliens

*Drugs **and** alcohol*

***Holy** war*

***Constructive** criticism*

*Prostitution is the world's oldest **profession**.*

*Porn **stars** who work in the **adult** film industry*

11.

Tolerance does not require much

"The difference between the right word and the almost right word is the difference between lightning and a lightning bug."

Mark Twain

* Tolerance does not require that you give up your hate, but compassion does;
* Tolerance does not require that you give up your desire to judge other people, but acceptance does;
* Tolerance does not require that you give up seeing other people as inferior, but equality does;
* Tolerance does not require that you value what others have to offer, but appreciating diversity does;
* Tolerance does not require that you treat people in a way that acknowledges their inherent worth, but respect does;
* Tolerance does not require that you challenge your faulty assumptions, but understanding does;
* Tolerance does not require that you do anything other than put up with people you disapprove of, but we are promoting it anyway. That seems to be setting the bar so low that rather than reaching for it, we are tripping over it.

12.
"I was just kidding"

Humor can be a tool of both tolerance and hatred. When you are not allowed to openly express your hostility toward people you disapprove of, you might feel that you are forced to tolerate them. What if you slip and let your disgust leak out? *"Oh, there goes another* (member of a group you don't like)." In response, a person you are with has the courage to confront your racist, sexist or homophobic remark by telling you that your comment was offensive. How do you respond? If you are not ready to acknowledge your prejudice, you might say *"I was just kidding! I can't believe you thought I was serious. Don't be so sensitive."*

Humor can be a way of expressing hostility without having to take responsibility for the attack. The person who explained his offensive remark in the above example, by claiming that he was just kidding, managed to express three insults in a single exchange. First, there was the original insult. Then, when he was confronted, he insulted the other person's intelligence (*"I can't believe you thought I was serious"* – i.e., you must be pretty stupid to think I was serious) and finally, criticized the reaction *("Don't be so sensitive."* – i.e., you have no right to feel the way you do, because you misperceived the situation).

The good news about the I-was-kidding approach is that people who say it are at least becoming aware that their attitude is no longer as acceptable as it perhaps once was. That's why they feel the need to deflect responsibility. The bad news is that they are deflecting responsibility because they are not yet ready to acknowledge the effect it has on others; nor are they ready to change their attitudes.

13.

Tolerance acts like a computer virus

When you pair tolerance with other concepts (e.g., *"we should promote understanding and tolerance,"* or *"we embrace increased acceptance, respect and tolerance,"*) those other terms protect tolerance from scrutiny. Since few would question the value of accepting people for who they are, or that we should be respectful of one another, or that it is good to strive to understand those who might be different from us, we automatically assume that tolerance must be good. (Otherwise, why would they be in the same sentence?) Those other terms serve to deactivate our radar, acting like bodyguards – protecting tolerance from close examination. The question that we should be shouting is *"Why are we going out of our way to protect 'tolerance'?"*

Another way to think of tolerance is as a virus. If you catch the flu bug, you do not concede defeat and decide simply to live with it. You do not reinterpret symptoms like a fever by saying, *"At least I have some nice color in my skin."* You do whatever is necessary to excise that virus from your system.

If your computer becomes infected with a virus, all of the otherwise valuable software is compromised. If you are unaware of the virus, you are surprised to find that your programs no longer work the way they should. The only solution is to identify and remove the virus before too much damage is done.

Tolerance is a conceptual virus that has infected many wonderful and well-intended people, programs and institutions. The solution is not to ignore it or to re-interpret it so that we can justify living with it. The solution is to acknowledge that it is there, recognize that it is harmful and make a commitment to remove it from our promotional campaigns, before too much damage is done. The risk of no longer promoting tolerance as a solution to hatred is non-existent. The risk of its continual promotion is immense. We can do better. We must do better. The time has come.

Exercise 3: Find and replace

Purpose: To demonstrate how adding "tolerance" to a list of positive concepts either adds nothing of value or actually undermines the message of the other terms.

Most computer word processors have a "find and replace" function that will search out words or phrases in a document (in this case, "tolerance") and replace them with another word or phrase (e.g., "acceptance" or "respect"). Find several statements promoting tolerance on websites, in brochures, or in books and try replacing tolerance with acceptance, respect or some other positive term, or just delete the word "tolerance" and see what happens to the meaning of the sentence. For example, in one of the phrases listed above "we should promote understanding and tolerance," might become "we should promote understanding and acceptance." You might find that by leaving out tolerance or replacing it with a more positive term, the message loses no value; it only becomes less ambiguous and problematic.

14.

Intent and impact of our use of language

"Tolerance, are you kidding? It's an insult. It's how white people feel better about themselves while continuing to hate Blacks."

Study participant

If people tell you that they are offended by a racial slur you uttered, do you correct them and tell them that you intended no harm and that they just do not understand your definition? Or do you acknowledge the impact of your words and use other words instead? A man, who was born in the 1920's, talked about how he used the "N" word to refer to black people. He noted that he meant it in a positive way and that black people should not be offended if he refers to them with that word. Did his alleged intent render the word harmless, by declassifying it as a racial slur? Is a black man who is offended by hearing him use the "N" word, wrong to feel that way? Or, if we are told that our language is hurtful, should we take those concerns seriously rather than defensively blame other people for misunderstanding us?

Likewise, if members of oppressed groups inform us that they are offended by our promotion of the word tolerance, should we inform them that the "correct" definition is the one proposed by UNESCO (the United Nations Educational, Scientific and Cultural Organization): *"Tolerance is respect, acceptance and appreciation of the rich diversity of our world's cultures, our forms of expression and ways of being human."* Therefore, we have no intention of changing our word selection? Perhaps not. Instead, we should re-examine our own hidden biases, and make a commitment to avoid the use of harmful language.

15.

Is tolerance even necessary?

"Education consists mainly of what we have unlearned."
Mark Twain

Imagine that we were successful in promoting acceptance, appreciation, understanding, love, compassion, justice, peace, respect, openness, inclusion, fairness and equality. Why would we need tolerance? Does it add anything positive not reflected in the others? I have yet to find someone who could identify even one positive contribution that tolerance makes that those other terms do not.

On the other hand, there is no shortage of people who can quickly identify negative, hurtful, condescending or insulting messages inherent in tolerance. So consider this question. What if we dropped tolerance from our list of proposed solutions to hatred, discrimination, prejudice and violence? What would be the risk? What would be the downside? What could we not accomplish? I have been waiting years for the answers to those questions. Since none seem to be forthcoming, it might be time for us to unlearn the alleged benefits of tolerance.

16.
Buddha's warning

As Buddha once advised:

"Do not believe in anything simply because you have heard it. Do not believe in anything simply because it is spoken and rumored by many. Do not believe in anything simply because it is found written in your religious books. Do not believe in anything merely on the authority of your teachers and elders. Do not believe in traditions because they have been handed down for many generations. But after observation and analysis, when you find that anything agrees with reason and is conducive to the good and benefit of one and all, then accept it and live up to it."

If we did not take his advice we would still believe that the world is flat, that no one will ever break the four-minute mile, that if humans were meant to fly, they would have been born with wings (O.K., for those of you who are afraid of flying, I'll give you that one), and that "separate but equal" guarantees quality education for black children. Fortunately, part of human nature is to question conventional wisdom. That inquisitive/challenging quality has been the basis for every innovation and creative solution.

The conventional wisdom seems to point in the direction of tolerance. It is time for us to challenge that "wisdom" assuming, of course, that we are ready to envision a better world in which tolerance and intolerance are replaced with acceptance and cooperation.

"A lie gets halfway around the world before the truth has a chance to get its pants on."
Sir Winston Churchill

17.

Promoting tolerance to fight hate is like prescribing aspirin to sick children

A frequent argument I hear by those still promoting tolerance as an antidote to hate is that not everyone is offended by tolerance. *"We realize it irritates many, but . . ." "Some people define tolerance in a positive way" "We've heard similar complaints about tolerance before, but not everyone agrees."* And so on.

To me that sounds remarkably similar to drug manufacturers defending products with dangerous side effects by citing studies that prove that the harm caused is statistically insignificant. (Insignificant that is, if you are not a family member of one of the deceased patients.) Those manufacturers have so much invested in their products that they might lose their objectivity and put profits before people's safety.

To offset that tendency, we have watchdog organizations such as the National Reye's Syndrome Foundation whose purpose, in their case, is to alert people to the dangers of giving aspirin to children or to pregnant mothers. (If you are a parent and are unaware of Reye's Syndrome, put down this book now and go to the Foundation's website or contact your doctor or pharmacist for important information.) The good news is that if your child has a fever, there are plenty of other medicines such as ibuprofen that do not increase the risk of getting Reyes. Now imagine if an "aspirin-advocacy" organization tried to tell you that not every child is harmed by aspirin, so they are going to keep promoting it, despite your objections. Clearly, that would be unacceptable.

I am afraid that this is what is happening with tolerance. It has been so widely promoted that we might feel we have too much invested to turn back now. I disagree with that assessment because we also had decades invested in the popular mantra *"separate but equal."* Eventually we realized what we now consider to be obvious – that separate was inherently unequal, and consequently, the highest court in our land struck it down.

It is time that we pay attention to the "warning labels" that are compiled in the pages of this book, appreciate the significant and harmful "side effects" of promoting tolerance, realize that there are ample and safe alternative concepts readily available for our use, and rid our mental medicine cabinets of the outdated prescription known as *"promoting tolerance."* We will all be healthier, happier and more peaceful for having done so.

18.

Pacifist or passivist?

*"The pacifist is as surely a traitor to his country
and to humanity as is the most brutal wrongdoer."*
Theodore Roosevelt

**If a pacifist is defined not by his belief in peace and
harmony but by his unwillingness to go to war, then
a warrior is defined not by what he fights for, but by
his unwillingness to live in peace and harmony.**

Do we really think that President Roosevelt meant that those who
believed in peace were traitors? If so, why would so many world leaders including U.S. presidents make the oxymoronic claim that we are
willing to "fight for peace?" It seems far more likely that President
Roosevelt meant "passivist," not "pacifist" but failed to understand the
difference.

A passivist (from the root word, "passive") is someone who is inactive, someone who does not stand up for his or her beliefs. A pacifist
(from the root word, "peace") is someone who believes in peace. The
words have nothing to do with each other. There are people who
believe in war who are passive, and others who are quite active. There
are people who believe in peace who are passive and others who are
quite active.

For example, Gandhi was a pacifist, but was by no means passive.
Through pacifist means, he repelled the entire British army out of
India. Not bad for a day's work (actually many days' work, requiring
extreme patience and persistence, but no violence). Likewise, Christ,
whom many refer to as the "Prince of Peace," was one of the greatest
pacifists of all time, yet by no means was he passive. Would President
Roosevelt (a Christian) consider Gandhi and Christ to be traitors to
humanity?

The real problem though is not that a single person (i.e., President Roosevelt) misunderstood the meaning of a word (e.g., pacifist or passivist). The problem is that enough other people have made that same mistake, so that some dictionaries are now defining a "passivist" as someone who believes in peace. The dangerous and misleading implication is that if you believe in peace, you are lazy, cowardly, unwilling to stand up for what you believe or to protect people you care about. Consequently, to prove that not to be true, you must be willing to do the opposite – strike out in violence, go to war, attack the enemy. This same confusion is happening with "tolerance." If enough people mistakenly believe it to be synonymous with acceptance, respect, or understanding, then we all feel compelled to proclaim its alleged virtue.

Both Christ and Gandhi, though, refused to fall prey to that illogic. They clearly demonstrated that being a pacifist requires courage, not cowardice and that pacifism can reap tremendous benefits for everyone involved. As Gandhi once said:

"I am prepared to die,
but there is no cause for which I am prepared to kill."

Sounds remarkably similar to Christ's story and what could be more courageous and loving than that?

19.

Action and adventure

Here is a homework assignment I give to students in my nonviolence classes to illustrate the power and importance of language:

Exercise 4: Action and adventure films

Purpose: To illustrate our tendency to use words to mask our attitudes or desires.

Walk into a movie rental store, and ask the clerk to suggest an action/adventure film that does not contain violence. Explain that you love action and adventure, but that you do not appreciate violence. You just don't want to watch a film that depicts someone being hurt. Wish the clerk luck, sit back, and enjoy watching the struggle. Notice how the clerk responds to your request and share your observations with others who have tried this exercise.

Once when I tried this exercise at my local Blockbuster store, a herd of five employees huddled in an attempt to find a nonviolent "action and adventure" film within their expansive collection. They failed.

The problem of course is that "action/adventure" is euphemistic for violence/destruction/pain/suffering. Why do we call it "action and adventure" rather than violence and destruction? Because we do not want to admit to ourselves or others that we want to watch a movie about violence. In contrast, who would fault us for wanting action and adventure in our lives?

The cost of this deception is that violent movies glamorize human suffering and desensitize us to the impact of violence. These consequences are magnified when it is not a movie you are watching, but a violent video game you are playing. Why? Because with the games you are not just a passive witness of the violence, you are an active participant, practicing as if you wanted to become a perpetrator of that violence.

Just for one day, I would like to be a criminal defense attorney representing a client who had been correctly charged with a violent assault. In defense of my client, I would challenge the prosecutor's assertion that my client acted with malicious intent. I would claim that he was merely seeking action and adventure in his life. I would then offer as evidence, the names of the last 25 "training videos" (a.k.a. action/adventure films or video games) that my client viewed or played. I would further suggest that since these movies have been approved for "mature" audiences, that my client, by mimicking the behavior in those films, must have been acting in a mature fashion. *"Your honor, at this point I ask that you dismiss all charges against my client."*

20.
Mental housecleaning

"Whatever words we utter should be chosen with care for people will hear them and be influenced by them for good or ill."

Buddha

A prominent civil rights organization, the Southern Poverty Law Center created a website and program devoted to addressing hatred, prejudice and discrimination. Parts of the website were labeled *"Digging deeper"* and *"Discovering our hidden biases."* They encouraged us to conduct self-examination. We all have biases, some of which are currently beyond our own awareness. These, of course, are the most dangerous, because we cannot see the harm that they cause. For example, in the *"Tolerant men treat women as equals"* section of this book, I address one of my own sexist attitudes that for years polluted my attempts to promote gender equality.

Another example comes from the U.S. Supreme Court, which took almost 60 years to rectify one of its own oppressive opinions. In 1896, it asserted that "separate but equal" was a valid concept in the Plessy v. Ferguson case. Not until 1954, in Brown v. Board of Education, did the Court acknowledge that separate was inherently unequal. We are now in the era of tolerance, when some believe that tolerance is a step toward equality. How long will it take us to recognize that tolerance, by its very nature, promotes inequality? When will we decide to abandon this condescending attitude and replace it with the plethora of alternative concepts (e.g., equality, respect, acceptance, understanding, appreciation, openness, inclusiveness, compassion, etc.) that do not share the negative connotations that characterize tolerance? What are we waiting for? It is time to do as the Southern Poverty Law Center suggested and dig deeper, discover our hidden biases, and move forward.

III.

Tolerance is intolerance

"Intolerance is the most socially acceptable form of egotism, for it permits us to assume superiority without personal boasting."

Sidney J. Harris
American journalist

"In working my steps, I've started to make amends for a life of intolerance. I've hurt a lot of people. But until now, I didn't realize that my "tolerant" attitude still allowed me to look down on people. Not very attractive, is it?"

Inmate at a County Correctional facility

I have asked literally hundreds of people *"Why tolerance?"* The most frequent answer involves their telling me how unacceptable intolerance is. Agreed, but their underlying assumption is that tolerance is not only a viable solution, but the best one because it is deemed to be the opposite of intolerance. In this chapter, we are going to challenge that assumption by examining closely the relationship between intolerance and tolerance. What we will find is that they are complementary rather than contradictory concepts. One cannot therefore be the solution for the other. Once we establish that, we will be ready for the next chapter, in which we will discuss how both tolerance and intolerance relate to hatred.

21.

Tolerance is the inhale, intolerance the exhale of hatred

Tolerance is no more effective in preventing intolerance than pulling back the sling is at preventing the shot.

A fire-breathing dragon is flying toward you. Would you be comforted by the dragon taking a deep breath, since as long as he inhales, no fire is launched in your direction? Quite the opposite. You would recognize that the inhale is the necessary preparation for the eventual attack. The deeper he inhales, the stronger the flame that will be blown in your direction. You cannot have one without the other. When we breathe, we alternate inhaling and exhaling. We do not think of inhaling as a solution to exhaling, or exhaling as a solution to inhaling. They complement each other. Without an inhalation, there is nothing to exhale. And until you exhale, there is no room for you to inhale any more air. If you hold your breath long enough while swimming under water, you soon focus on nothing other than your next opportunity to breathe, so that the longer you hold your breath, the more frantically you gasp when you finally come up for air.

The same reasoning can be applied to hatred. You inhale tolerance and exhale intolerance. Tolerance is hatred inhaling and then holding its breath. But holding your breath does not make it less likely that you want to exhale. Quite the opposite. It makes your eventual exhale that much more emphatic and desperate. Tolerance is no more the solution to hatred, than inhaling is the solution to breathing. Tolerance appears to be the short term solution to intolerance because you cannot do both simultaneously, anymore than you can inhale and exhale at the same time. Tolerance only appears to be the solution. In reality, tolerance and intolerance are two elements of an ever-so-vicious cycle of hatred and violence.

22.

Intolerance teaches tolerance

*"I have learnt silence from the talkative, toleration from the intolerant,
and kindness from the unkind; yet strange,
I am ungrateful to these teachers."*

Kahlil Gibran

I too am ungrateful to those who demonstrate harmful behaviors such as intolerance. One of the reasons is that I might quickly assume that the opposite of intolerance is tolerance, similar to assuming that the opposite of love is hate. But I would be wrong on both accounts. You have probably heard the expression "a love-hate relationship." Love and hate can co-exist in a relationship, because rather than being opposites, they are both intense reactions to another person. The opposite of love is not hate but the absence of love, or indifference. Similarly, the opposite of intolerance is not tolerance. They can both be intense experiences of hatred; the difference is only in their expression - intolerance is an overt expression, tolerance, a covert expression.

The danger in thinking of tolerance and intolerance as opposites is that we might be misled to think that tolerance is the correct disposal of hatred rather than the destructive hiding of that toxic attitude.

23.

Stuck in traffic

"Tolerance brings up the idea that people who tolerate you can withdraw it . . . . Tolerance can easily slip into intolerance."

Professor Rinaldo Walcott
Associate Professor
Department of Sociology and Equity Studies in Education
University of Toronto

One way to think of tolerance is that it is intolerance being held up at a stop light. The longer you are stuck there, the more frustrated you get, because you have not yet arrived at your destination. Tolerance is not an end point. It is what we might do in the meantime until we can "put up with it no longer." The question is: What will we do when that time comes? Our hope is that the object of our tolerance will just go away or change so that our discomfort will be relieved. But what if that does not happen? What if the other person or group of people we are tolerating does not change or disappear? What will we do when our tolerance runs out?

24.

Complementary not contradictory

Tolerance is what you do while waiting for the right time to be intolerant.

Imagine a bicycle wheel with only two spokes. One emanates horizontally from the hub forward. The other emanates horizontally backward. They appear to be pointing in opposite directions, until you consider the context. Once the wheel starts to move we can see that the spokes are not really opposites; rather, they are moving in the same direction (i.e., forward when the bicycle is moving in that direction, backward when the bicycle is backing up) merely taking turns which is in front of the other.

Similarly, tolerance and intolerance take turns. They are complementary – intolerance when violent acts are committed, tolerance when they are not. Tolerance is the escalating resentment, planning and preparation stage; intolerance is the implementation stage, acting on the plan that was devised while the situation was becoming intolerable.

25.

Neither tolerance nor intolerance

Being repulsed by intolerance does not mean that you endorse tolerance. You do not confront people who shout racial slurs by asking them to whisper instead.

Try this exercise from a workshop on challenging oppressive attitudes and behavior.

Exercise 5: Neither tolerance nor intolerance

Purpose: To challenge a common misconception that tolerance is the opposite of intolerance and therefore a viable solution to hate.

Imagine that there is a group of people who disgust you, whom you disapprove of, maybe even hate. You are not allowed to commit violent acts of intolerance. Nor can you enslave them, ostracize them or make them go away. A natural reaction would be to feel that you have no choice but to tolerate them. But imagine for a moment that tolerance was also forbidden. Now what? What else could you do?

Sometimes when I conduct this exercise, there is a prolonged period of silence in the room as people struggle to think of even one alternative. Eventually though, the solutions start to surface with some groups being able to generate 15 or 20 constructive and practical alternatives. See how many occur to you.

26.

Opposites attract

"It's too late for me. Everyone I know is racist and homophobic.
I probably always will be. But it's not too late for my son.
I don't want school to teach him that being tolerant is good enough.
I don't want him thinking he's better than someone because of his race.
I want him to learn acceptance."

Study participant

Tolerance and intolerance appear to be opposites, just as sensitive and insensitive are opposites. But word construction does not always paint an accurate picture. Consider flammable and inflammable. Opposites, right? Wrong. They actually mean the same thing. They both mean the ability to combust. As another example, consider the word "near." "Near perfect" means, not perfect, but close to being perfect. "Near-death" experience? Close to without actually being dead. What about a "near miss"? Parallel construction would suggest that that should mean that it was not a miss, but was close to being a miss. However, it means just the opposite. It means that it actually was a miss, but was close to being a hit.

The point is that we need to be careful with language. Words and phrases do not always mean what we think they should mean. We might think that tolerance is the opposite of or solution to intolerance since its structure seems to imply opposition. We think that since intolerance is connected to hatred, then tolerance must be connected to the opposite of hatred. Upon closer inspection though, we can notice that intolerance is not the presence of hatred; it is the overt expression of hatred. Therefore, the opposite of overtly expressing hatred is either the covert expression of hatred or the (temporary) choice not to express hatred. Hatred, disgust or disapproval is still present. The person who is feeling that hatred is just holding it in, keeping it private, for now.

27.

Don't pull the trigger! A lesson in gun safety

> What is the difference between tolerance and intolerance? Tolerance has a silencer attached to the end of the barrel.

Imagine you are pointing a loaded gun (hatred) at someone's head. Now you need to decide whether it is better for you to pull the trigger (an act of intolerance) or not pull the trigger (an act of tolerance). Of course, the "tolerant" act is better than the intolerant one, but it leaves a far more important question unanswered (and perhaps even unasked). Why is it that you are pointing a gun at someone's head in the first place? Is it harmless to point a gun as long as you don't pull the trigger? Nonviolence is not refusing to pull the trigger. Nonviolence is refusing to pick up the gun.

I once worked with a man in a domestic violence program who had inserted both barrels of a shotgun into his wife's mouth because (a) he thought she had cheated on him, and (b) he felt entitled to coerce a confession from her, by whatever means necessary. According to him, he told her *"Confess your sins, admit that you slept around, and I'll blow your brains out and we'll call it even."* When I asked him if he thought his behavior was abusive, he said without hesitation *"Absolutely not! How could it have been abusive? The gun wasn't even loaded."*

He later claimed, *"With all that I've had to tolerate from this woman, the fact that I didn't load the gun shows just how much I loved her. So who is the real victim here?"* Sometimes we view tolerance (e.g., unloaded gun) as a gift, because we compare it to worse alternatives (e.g., loaded gun). We seem to forget that putting a gun into someone's mouth, even without firing, is harmful enough. Similarly, is tolerance harmless because you have made a (temporary) decision not to be intolerant, or is it harmful due to the ever-present and underlying hatred, disgust or disapproval that fuels the perceived need for tolerance?

28.

Tolerance is a snap shot; intolerance, a movie

Hit the pause button in the middle of playing back a movie and you are left viewing a single frame. You see a very small sample, but you know that there are scenes that lead up to that point and scenes that follow. Eventually, you push the "play" button to find out what happens next.

Tolerance is the single frame you see if you depress the pause button while viewing a movie on hatred and oppression. You know that the story line contains scenes of hostility, condescension or disapproval that led to the choice to be tolerant. You also know that there are other scenes to follow. Tolerance is neither the end of the movie, nor does it change the theme or direction of the story. Once you resume the movie, the hostility continues. Rather than encouraging hateful people to repeatedly hit the pause button (as we do when we suggest that they become more tolerant) it is time for us to find a different movie to watch.

29.

Tolerance is the eye of the storm

Tolerance is an inactive volcano. But make no mistake; it is still a volcano.

Among battered women's advocates, there is frequent talk about the cycle of violence. This cycle is described as consisting of three stages: tension building, violence and the honeymoon period. One of the problems with this metaphor is the naming of the honeymoon stage. An actual honeymoon is a celebration of a wonderful event (i.e., a wedding). So what wonderful event is being celebrated during this period of nonviolence in the cycle of violence? Should the victim celebrate not being hit? Should the perpetrator be thanked for such a "generous" cessation of hostility? I think not. The absence of violence should be considered a given, not viewed as an extraordinary effort, worthy of celebration.

A better metaphor for this period of non-violence in a relationship marred by recurring violence or abuse is the eye of the storm. For those who have had the experience of being in the eye of a hurricane, they report noticing how calm it is. The eye is sunny, no wind, no clear sign that a hurricane recently hit, and no indication that the back side of the storm will soon arrive. Even though the weather is calm, this is not a time to relax. Instead, it is a time for hyper-vigilance, wondering when the storm will strike again. This is how victims of domestic violence often describe their experience. They know the abuser will attack again, especially if it has happened many times before. They just don't always know when or how or how bad the next attack will be.

If we view acts of intolerance as a violent storm, then tolerance is the eye of that storm. It is the period during which the "tolerant" person is not actively attacking; the violence is in remission. But there is always the promise of the next attack. The objects of that tolerance never feel accepted as equals because the air of condescension surrounds the "gift" of tolerance. Consequently, they realize that those in power can withdraw their tolerance whenever they see fit. At that point, the storm of intolerance returns, often more violent or oppressive than it was initially. Even if the next attack never actually occurs, the disapproving attitude, inherent in tolerance, is oppressive enough.

30.

Every supremacist is tolerant

What do you call a supremacist who is disciplined enough to keep a secret? Tolerant.

What would supremacists look like who were never tolerant? They would lash out every time they were exposed to the objects of their hate, since not lashing out would be a tolerant act. Supremacists spend the majority of their time in tolerance mode. This consists of either resenting society's insistence that they tolerate people they disapprove of or planning their next attack, or more likely, both.

For them, tolerance is not the solution to intolerance; it is the precursor to it. Being "forced" into tolerance is what supremacists cite as justification for their hatred and violence. It is time for us to challenge that justification by offering compelling alternatives.

Exercise 6: Hate group language

Purpose: To expose how pervasive the language and attitude of tolerance is within hate groups.

Examine the text of several sermons, speeches, newsletter articles or blog entries that were written by members of hate groups. See how long it takes for you to find phrases such as "We're not going to tolerate this infestation of foreigners anymore, are we!" What do you suppose would happen if you suggested that they practice even more tolerance? How successful do you think you would be in motivating them to give up their hatred?

Discuss with your classmates, colleagues, family or friends what kind of conversation you might want to have with people who resent having to be tolerant. How could you reassure them that being different is not the same as being bad or dangerous? Imagine starting your conversation with "You don't have to 'tolerate' people you disapprove of. I have a better idea." What would you say next? See if you can make suggestions that involve respect, appreciation, acceptance or understanding.

31.

The lesser of two evils is still evil

New Hampshire ramped up its domestic violence prevention efforts in 1993 in response to a criminal court case. The defendant in that case had severely physically abused his wife. The judge, while addressing the defendant's inexcusable behavior asked *"Don't you think a slap would have been sufficient?"* While the judge was correct that a slap causes less damage than a severe beating, he was obviously incorrect and irresponsible to suggest that slapping is acceptable. Instead, he should have clearly confronted the defendant's belief that he was justified in using any form of violence or abuse to control his partner.

Similarly, though tolerance (postponing an attack on the object of your hate or disgust) is less harmful than intolerance (currently attacking what or whom you hate), does not mean that we should promote tolerance. Instead, we should challenge the belief that it is either necessary, acceptable, or that you are entitled to, hate a certain group of people in the first place.

IV.

Tolerance and hatred

"Tolerance has not led to the formation of a healthy, interdependent community, but rather a country divided by walls of tolerance, only occasionally crossed and usually for destructive purposes. Tolerance has not protected us from acts of hate but rather cast us in a frozen state of societal fragmentation with no apparent change in sight."

Victor Kazanjian
Dean of Religious and Spiritual Life, Wellesley College

Apparently, the "walls of tolerance" referred to in the above quotation, are not just metaphorical. There is an actual "Wall of Tolerance" in Montgomery, Alabama. If your goal is to promote equality, unity and inclusion, would a wall really be the best symbol? Did we not recently tear one down in Germany due to both its practical and symbolic significance? What about the "Iron Curtain?" Were we not pleased to see that fall?

Perhaps given the condescending nature of tolerance, a "wall" of tolerance was inevitable, despite what I'm sure were the best of intentions. If those commissioned to design a structure were asked to build something indicative of inclusion, connectedness or community rather than tolerance, a wall certainly would have been ruled out as the symbol.

Before we discuss effective strategies for addressing hatred we need to understand why tolerance is not only ineffective, but can actually be counterproductive (as was suggested by the above quotation).

In this chapter, we will explore how tolerance is an ever-present part of a hateful person's experience. We will see that while some civil rights advocates have promoted tolerance in an effort to *eliminate* hatred, oppressors have felt that the promotion of tolerance has *fueled* their hatred!

32.

Tolerance: Polite hatred

Emily Post would be proud. You are at a formal dinner party and the bean dip is not agreeing with you. You feel the pressure, but do not want to succumb to the almost irresistible urge to pass gas. You excuse yourself to find a more private setting to seek relief.

Those who harbor hatred are posed with a similar problem. Hatred can be violent, scary, and ugly. Its overt expression has increasingly been met with social disapproval. It is far more acceptable to keep their hostility to themselves, at least until they are in a more private setting where they can express their disgust to like-minded souls.

Tolerance is politically correct hatred, a conduct disorder on medication. It is the public mask that supremacists wear to keep their attitudes from being detected by the casual observer. As with the intestinal discomfort, they can try to resist the urge to express their hatred or they can search for a more permanent solution by preventing the buildup of hatred in the first place. They can ask themselves why it is that they feel so threatened by individual and group differences and why they feel a need to make others conform to their way of being. You might have a favorite color in the rainbow, but something of value would surely be lost if there were no other colors. Indeed, there would be no rainbow.

33.

Promoting the wrong solution makes the problem worse

"Capacity to endure pain or hardship"
"Physiological resistance to a toxin"
"The ability of an organism to resist or survive infection by a parasitic or pathogenic organism"
Dictionary definitions of tolerance

There are many websites and programs extolling the virtues of tolerance and suggesting that its promotion is the most effective way to fight hate. The problem is that those who hate, already feel that they have been forced to "put up with" (i.e., tolerate) too much already. Suggesting to them that they should tolerate even more, just makes matters worse. For example, if you go to the hospital after getting food poisoning from a restaurant, the doctors will not suggest that you learn to tolerate it. Instead, they will help you rid your body of the toxin and suggest that you not return to that restaurant until the food has been cleared for safety.

By promoting tolerance, we fail to challenge the belief that a certain group of people is toxic. We are in effect telling the haters to go back to the restaurant to eat more poisonous food. Why on earth would they want to comply with that directive? Shoving tolerance down their throats would only increase their resentment and eventual hostility. It would be far better to challenge their assumption that the targets of their hatred are people to be feared or despised. Only when they realize that group differences are not by their very nature toxic or dangerous, will they be able to truly accept people who may look, think, worship or act differently.

Exercise 7: The effect of promoting tolerance on oppressors

Purpose: To expose one of the dangers of promoting a condescending attitude.

Consider the following statement. "*The greatest problem with promoting tolerance is that by doing so, we elevate the oppressor's escalating resentment to the level of a virtue allowing him to view himself as the victim of the person he oppresses. This provides even more justification for his eventual attack when his tolerance runs out.*" *What does this statement mean? Do you agree? Why or why not? Do you think that oppressors actually feel victimized by those they oppress? If so, then what do you think we should do (instead of promoting more tolerance) to encourage those who abuse their power to give up their oppressive tactics? How can we help them to feel less resentful?*

34.

Tolerance creates mutual resentment

"Tolerance . . . is the lowest form of human cooperation. It is the drab, uncomfortable halfway house between hate and charity."

Rev. Robert I. Gannon, S.J.
Former President, Fordham University

Those who tolerate, resent having to put up with the objects of their hatred, while those being tolerated resent the condescending attitude. Have you ever heard a black man say, *"All I really want is for Whites to tolerate me?"* Or have you heard a woman say *"If men would just tolerate me in the workplace, I would be content?"* And yet, while oppressed people are clear that they do not want tolerance, those in a position of power are "generously" offering it to them.

35.

Tolerance should not be our "rule of thumb"

Most of us have heard the phrase "rule of thumb," which refers to a heuristic or guideline that we follow in a particular situation. Not as many people know the phrase's history. One of the early uses of that phrase dates back to Colonial America. It referred to allowable forms of physical violence a man could use to "discipline" his wife. Since women were considered to have less status than men (e.g., they were not allowed to vote or own property) they were viewed as men's property, much like children. Consequently, the "man of the house" was responsible for the actions of others in his household. If he believed that his wife or children misbehaved, then it was considered to be both his right and responsibility to discipline (i.e., punish) them until they behaved appropriately. Often the discipline included physical violence. This practice was generally accepted because what a man did in the privacy of his own home was considered no one's business but his own.

But what if he got carried away and severely beat his wife? What if she needed medical attention? What if she died? What if the neighbors could not help but notice and be concerned about what was happening inside his house? No one wanted to go into another man's home and tell him how to treat his family members, but they could not ignore extreme forms of violence. The solution was to draw a line between appropriate and inappropriate forms of discipline. That is where the rule of thumb came in. That rule suggested that a man was allowed to beat his wife as long as the stick he used to strike her was no thicker than his thumb. On the surface, the rule of thumb appeared to be an attempt to protect women from severe beatings. But more accurately, it condoned wife abuse. Effectively, it provided an instruction manual for men who wanted to beat their wives. It did nothing to confront the belief that men were entitled to strike, abuse, or otherwise control women. It did nothing to address gender inequality. It merely asked men to be subtle enough so that society could look the other way and not get involved.

The relationship between the rule of thumb and a husband's violence is analogous to the relationship between tolerance and hatred.

Tolerance does not confront the underlying and destructive belief that one group of people is superior to another, it merely asks those who feel superior to be subtle enough (i.e., tolerant) that society does not have to intervene on behalf of those who are being oppressed.

36.

Tolerance is used to justify misogyny and domestic violence

Consider the problem of domestic violence. Male batterers demonstrate their misogyny by using the judgmental language of tolerance. By describing what they have to tolerate from women, they try to justify their use of violence. *"If she would just do what I tell her to do, I wouldn't have to hit her."* *"All women are the same. They know how to push your buttons until you can't take it anymore and you just have to teach them a lesson."*

Consequently, tolerance makes perpetrators feel better about themselves through their sense of achievement (*"Look at what I have had to put up with!"*). By allowing batterers to hold onto this false sense of superiority, tolerance makes equality between men and women impossible.

37.

Stalkers are experts in tolerance

Stalking is to battering as tolerance is to intolerance. Stalking is what perpetrators do when they are not allowed contact with their targets. Battering is what they do when they gain access. Likewise, tolerance is what haters do when they are not allowed to strike. Intolerance is what they do when they finally do strike.

When batterers are issued a restraining order due to the threat they pose to their victims, we do not want them to "tolerate" the fact that they cannot have contact. Tolerance keeps them focused on what they cannot have. When they can no longer tolerate being apart from their family, they will attempt to violate that restraining order (which happens far too often). Instead, we want them to *respect* the court's decision, *understand* why it is in place and *accept* the current situation. We want them to shift their focus away from tracking down their victims to changing their abusive behavior and the inflated sense of entitlement and privilege that fuels it.

38.

Tolerance is hatred subject to a restraining order

Victims of domestic violence often seek restraining orders when they are afraid for their physical safety due to the abusive actions of their partner. These "protective" orders, issued by a court, tell the abuser to stay away from the victim. The orders do not force abusers to give up their desire to control, manipulate or hurt the victim; they merely tell them to stay away and enhance the penalties if they were to have unauthorized contact. In some cases, the abuser resents this restriction, and lashes out against the victim in retaliation (as evidenced by domestic homicides that occur while a restraining order is in effect).

Tolerance is very similar to a restraining order. It does nothing to encourage acceptance, appreciation, respect or understanding. Tolerance merely prohibits acts of intolerance. But as with domestic violence restraining orders, perpetrators might eventually decide that *"I can't put up with it any more"* and lash out even more viciously than they did before they were told that they should be tolerant.

I am not suggesting that we should stop issuing restraining orders to batterers. They can and often do enhance safety for victims and accountability for offenders, at least in the short term. But as the name implies, they *restrain* batterers from doing what they really want to do. This is the point with the promotion of tolerance. It attempts to *restrain* hateful people from doing what they really want to do rather than encourage them to give up their hate. I have never heard a batterer tell me that a restraining order taught him to respect women. That is what batterer intervention programs are designed to do. However, I have heard several tell me that restraining orders did teach them to be more careful so that they wouldn't get caught the next time they were abusive. I don't think we should teach hateful people, through the promotion of tolerance, to become more careful so that they don't get caught being oppressive. Teaching them how to be 'tolerant oppressors' is not a step in the right direction. It only helps them to become more subtle so that they can avoid detection.

39.

Forgiveness is a cure for tolerance

"To understand everything is to forgive everything."

*"You will not be punished for your anger,
you will be punished by your anger."*
Buddha

*"Hate is too great a burden to bear.
It injures the hater more than it injures the hated."*
Coretta Scott King

Forgiveness is the art of letting go of your anger. In contrast, tolerance is the suppression of your anger so that you can pretend that it is not there. But it is still there, festering, polluting your consciousness, weakening your soul.

After Pope John Paul II was shot in May of 1981, he talked about the need to give up his hatred of the assailant. Yes, forgiveness is part of his job description, so you might think that giving up hatred was easy and natural for him. That is not, however, how he spoke of it. He focused on his own need to give up his hatred, because he believed that hatred often hurts the one feeling it even more than it hurts the target of the hatred. At no point did he suggest that giving up the hatred was due to a decision to be tolerant of the person who harmed him or of that person's violent act. Becoming more tolerant would have only frozen the hatred in place, creating a heavy burden for the Pope to carry. The act of forgiveness freed him from the burden of tolerance.

40.

Tolerance is hatred in remission

Tolerance is the camouflage that hatred uses to look like acceptance.

When a disease is in remission, the patient is asymptomatic. It is difficult to determine if the person even has the disease. But having a disease that is in remission is not the same as being cured. The disease is still there. There are just no obvious outward manifestations. Consider herpes for example. Between outbreaks, the patient does not notice any symptoms; but not only is the person still infected with the disease, that person can still spread the disease even during remission.

Similarly, tolerance is a way to make hatred appear to be in remission. But while overt acts of intolerance are absent, the underlying condescending attitude might persist and can easily be spread to others through jokes, propaganda, disapproving looks, tone of voice, etc. The only way to "cure" the disease is to examine why it is that we think it is appropriate or beneficial to dislike or fear groups of people. Until we can truly accept and even appreciate our differences (rather than feel threatened by them) hatred and its destructive expression will continue to pollute and threaten our society.

41.

Tolerance is a symptom of hatred, not a solution to it

"John hates Bill." An overwhelming 94 percent of our study participants thought that tolerance was the most natural reaction John would have to someone he hated (rather than thinking that tolerance was something to strive for). If tolerance were the solution or alternative to hatred, we would say that now that John has learned tolerance, he *no longer* hates Bill, just the opposite of what we found.

42.
Tolerance teaches hatred

Tolerance applies only to things you do not like (i.e., if you like something, it makes no sense to tolerate it; you are too busy appreciating it.). So imagine you are a young student in elementary school and your teacher addresses how we should treat people who are different from us. You have never met and know very little about some racial, ethnic, or social group, so you have no idea how you feel about them. But you are told that you should show them tolerance. Since tolerance only applies to negative things, the implication is that you should not like them (otherwise tolerance would be irrelevant or unnecessary).

When you finally meet one of these people, you already "know" that there is something wrong with them. You have no idea what that something is, but somehow you are better than they are. If you want to feel good about yourself, you will be tolerant. If they, in turn resent your tolerance (i.e., perhaps due to its condescending overtones) their hostility proves to you that indeed there is something wrong with them. It is not much better if they do not express hostility, because then your condescending attitude goes entirely unchallenged. You walk away feeling good about yourself; they walk away feeling worse about themselves and worse about you as well.

Imagine how much better the world would be if instead of teaching our children that they should be tolerant of those who are different, we taught them that they should embrace our commonalities and celebrate our marvelous differences. How much unnecessary and destructive fear would we cleanse from our collective consciousness?

43.

National Brotherhood Week

In 1965, Tom Lehrer, a musical comedian performed a skit, *"National Brotherhood Week,"* addressing the relationship between hatred and tolerance. In the skit, he exposed racial, economic class and religious tensions with specific mention of anti-Semitism and hostility toward those with disabilities. What follows is some of the lyrics and how they connect to hatred, discrimination, prejudice and tolerance:

"It's fun to eulogize the people you despise, as long as you don't let 'em in your school." (segregation)

"Step up and shake the hand of someone you can't stand. You can tolerate him if you try." (connection between hatred and tolerance)

"Be nice to people who are inferior to you." (supremacist attitude)

"It's only for a week, so have no fear. Be grateful that it doesn't last all year." (acknowledgment that tolerance is time-limited and not a long-term solution to hatred. The question then, is: What happens at the end of National Brotherhood Week, when your tolerance runs out?)

Exercise 8:   Search the media

Purpose: To develop an appreciation for the significant role that the media plays in reflecting, reinforcing and shaping our values, specifically with regard to tolerance.

"National Brotherhood Week" was created in the 1960's. See if you can find other, perhaps more recent skits, songs, TV shows or movies that address the attitude of tolerance and how it relates to hatred, prejudice or discrimination. What message does each try to convey about the meaning and impact of tolerance? If you are a musician, song writer, playwright or poet, compose your own work addressing the impact of tolerance on our relationships with others.

44.
Defense of marriage

"We should not tolerate the attack on marriage by homosexuals."

A twice divorced, heterosexual man

Traditional marriage is indeed in need of defense. For example, in the U.S. the current divorce rate is over 50 %, definitely a failing grade. When you also consider the percentage of marriages that are unhappy or dysfunctional, but do not end in divorce due to religious beliefs, concerns about the children, finances, reactions from friends and family, etc., the failure rate is much higher. Why? The reasons are many and varied including: unrealistic expectations, stresses of modern living, changing values, domestic and sexual violence, infidelity, communication problems, and many others.

In 1996, the Defense of Marriage Act was passed in the U.S. You would think that legislation with that name would address the issues listed above that are contributing to the disintegration of so many marriages. But you would be wrong. The bill was designed to "protect" traditional marriage from an attack launched by homosexuals. Come again? I have never heard heterosexual couples express concern that their marriage was in jeopardy because two men or two women down the street also wanted to get married. Why would sharing an institution such as marriage with people of a different sexual orientation, threaten the quality or existence of your own marriage? How does sharing the basic civil rights that emanate from marriage threaten heterosexual couples? These are difficult questions to answer.

In reality, traditional marriage is not being attacked and therefore is not what is being defended. It is only traditional marriage *as a monopoly* (accessible only by heterosexuals) that is being protected. If such a bill were proposed in the business, rather than the personal world, it would be considered an unfair business practice and banned by antitrust provisions. The same protections (for non-heterosexuals) should apply here.

I once spoke with a married heterosexual man who expressed "extreme concern" when he heard the words "gay" and "marriage" in the same sentence. I asked him an unexpected question. *"How do you suppose your own marriage would suffer if heterosexuals lost their monopoly on that institution?"* He immediately informed me that my question was stupid and changed the topic. When I saw him again several weeks later, he apologized for his reaction and told me that he actually thought that my question was a good one. The problem, he said, was that he did not have a very good answer. It made him wonder why gay people caused him such discomfort and why he was so scared to grant them equal access to marriage.

I explained to him how I viewed heterosexuals sharing marriage with other orientations. To me it was like a lit candle sharing its flame with an unlit one. The act of sharing does not cause the glow of the first candle to diminish in the least; it only makes the whole room brighter. Then, if the flame of the first candle were to go out, a new ally would be standing by to offer assistance.

Exercise 9: Defense of marriage

Purpose: To expose a common tactic of oppression (i.e., making an act of oppression appear to be a justifiable, if not honorable, self-defense strategy) and to encourage the development of constructive responses to oppression.

Rather than spending time, energy and other resources trying to exclude a group of people from marriage, heterosexuals should focus on improving the success rate of their own marriages.

Try drafting alternate legislation, public policy, or educational programming that would serve to "defend" marriage from what is truly threatening that institution (e.g., abuse, infidelity, lack of commitment, artificial and unrealistic goals, poor communication, etc.). See if you can find a way to include (rather than exclude) couples who are not heterosexuals. Consider the candle analogy in this section. How can people of all sexual orientations work together to strengthen marriage? What is the advantage of seeing people with a different orientation as part of the solution, rather than characterizing them as a threat or part of the problem?

45.

Hatred needs tolerance to survive

Tolerance is the cure for segregation is the cure for tolerance.

Tolerance fills the void created by the outlawing of slavery and segregation. Tolerance helps to maintain de facto segregation, now that de jure segregation has been removed. For hatred to survive and thrive, it needs people to defend tolerance. If you are not allowed to attack, enslave, or segregate those you despise, your only option is to tolerate them. But what if tolerance were no longer considered an acceptable option? What could you do? You could accept them for who they are, opening up a wonderful world of understanding, respect, appreciation and peaceful coexistence.

V.

Conflict resolution

Conflict can range from a mild disagreement between friends to international war. The parties involved can have equal status and power or there can be one party that clearly dominates or oppresses the other. In either event, what is meant by the resolution of that conflict? Does it necessarily mean that both parties are satisfied with the outcome or does it merely suggest a cessation of outward hostility? What role does tolerance play? What method of conflict resolution does tolerance most closely resemble? Does tolerance lead to the satisfaction of both, just one, or neither of the parties involved?

In this chapter we will answer these questions as we explore how a tolerant attitude affects some of our everyday struggles.

46.

Peel your own banana

Immigrants who went through Ellis Island upon arriving in America, were fed a welcome meal. Some of the food they were given was unfamiliar to them, such as bananas. What they did know about a banana was that it was a fruit. They also knew that many fruits have edible outsides and inedible seeds or pits on the inside (e.g., apricots, grapes, cherries). Applying this logic to the unfamiliar banana, some of them ate the not-so-tasty fibrous peel and threw away the surprisingly large, soft "seed" on the inside. Not a pleasant experience.

Fortunately, most of us have no such difficulties when presented with a banana. We do not need anyone to separate the peel from the fruit or to tell us which part is edible. We also do not normally resent someone for giving us the inedible part. In fact, we probably prefer that they do not handle the fruit directly. We are more than capable of discarding the part we do not want or need.

So what if we applied that same set of skills to our communication with others. For example, someone is upset with us for showing up late for an appointment. But rather than just tell us why they are upset (the fruit), they also raise their voice or use harsh language (the inedible peel). What if we listened to the important part and threw away the rest, rather than perpetuate a vicious cycle by getting upset with them for their communication style or choices? If you lash back, you are being intolerant. If you silently resent their attack, you are being tolerant. If you know when to peel the banana yourself, you are practicing acceptance and are more likely to be happier, healthier and stress-free. This does not mean that you either condone or appreciate their aggressiveness. It only means that you are choosing to focus on what you have control over, and discarding the rest.

47.

Setting boundaries and resolving conflict

Winning an argument is no more possible than winning a car accident. Everyone suffers.

Tolerance is what you might do when you cannot or will not set boundaries. Setting appropriate boundaries involves allowing others to do as they wish as long as it does not hurt you. If you do not know how to set boundaries, you might feel that you have to either attack the other person or tolerate their behavior. It is far better to recognize a respectful middle ground than to feel that tolerance and intolerance are your only options. That is the essence of successful conflict resolution.

Conflict resolution strategies can be divided into three categories: passive (i.e., ignoring your own welfare while allowing others to get their way), aggressive (i.e., ignoring others' welfare while focusing only on getting your own needs met) and assertive (i.e., focusing on getting your needs met, but being careful not to hurt others in the process). Tolerance is the passive approach; intolerance, the aggressive approach. Neither is a healthy way of resolving conflict.

The assertive approach is far more respectful, with the goal of mutual acceptance. *"You accept me for who I am, and I will accept you for who you are. If we have differences, our goal is to make sure that each of us gets some of what we want. Neither of us exploits, manipulates, dominates or controls the other. We can be different, but neither of us is better than the other; we are presumed equal, with an equal right to be happy."*

Exercise 10: Assertiveness as an alternative to tolerance

Purpose: To practice differentiating between healthy and unhealthy responses to conflict. To illustrate how tolerant (i.e., passive) approaches are not the healthiest options.

Imagine your spouse asks you to spend the afternoon doing something you really do not enjoy (e.g., going to the opera, to a football game, shopping, etc.). In response, you say either:

"What a waste of time! I can't believe that you want to drag me to (the unpleasant activity). Go by yourself." Or

"Fine (even though it is not really fine to you). When do we have to go? (You ask this while trying to mask your resentment. You figure it's just not worth an argument, so you go along with it like you usually do.)

Which of these responses is aggressive (intolerant) and which is passive (tolerant)?

What would be an assertive response?

Why is the assertive response healthier for both you and the relationship than the ones in which you are being tolerant or intolerant?

48.

A tiny pebble in your shoe

I am often asked *"Isn't tolerance O.K. at least for the trivial matters?"* I guess it is, but I think that misses the point when discussing whether or not to promote tolerance. You could also say that it is "O.K." to occasionally have a bad day. Not only is that true, it is inevitable; we all have bad days. That does not mean, however, that we should promote having bad days. In contrast, we strive to minimize the occurrence of bad days and their impact on our lives. The same is true of tolerance. Occasionally feeling tolerant does not automatically convert someone into a white supremacist; on the other hand, it is hard to imagine why anyone would strive to experience it. Tolerance, even in the trivial cases, feels like a pebble in the shoe. The pebble will not cause serious damage, but it will bother you until you remove it. And once it is gone, you certainly do not seek to replace it.

One advantage of the trivial situations is that the stakes are so low that there is little risk in practicing healthy assertiveness. If the other person does not respond in a positive way, it is no big deal. You still get to walk away knowing that you engaged them respectfully. No one can take that away from you. These small opportunities also allow you to safely practice the skill of assertiveness so when you really do need it for the major problems, you will be better prepared to handle the potentially stressful interaction. If instead, you choose to be passively tolerant, you miss the chance for personal growth and enhanced intimacy in your relationships and are likely left with a feeling of resentment. You also deprive the other person of the chance to get to know you and what you need.

Exercise 11: The week in review

Purpose: To learn a simple strategy for managing relationship conflict that avoids the need to endure the discomfort of tolerance.

In our classes on non-violence, we discuss several assertive strategies for maintaining healthy relationships. We often hear someone say "My spouse did something annoying, but it wasn't a big deal, so I just let it go." The next week, the spouse reportedly did something else irritating and then another. But each time, "It wasn't worth fighting about." After a while the resentment created by these small annoyances builds up until the person "can't tolerate it anymore" and ends up in a three-hour argument about who is supposed to take out the garbage on Wednesday nights.

How could fights like this be avoided? One technique you might want to try in your own relationships is what we call "The week in review." This involves periodic conversations at a mutually convenient time that lasts only a few minutes. Each partner has an opportunity to say what they liked about the relationship over the past week and what they would like to be different. For this to be helpful, (1) both partners must be interested in doing this (i.e., you cannot force or coerce the other person to participate), (2) they should mention first what they liked, then discuss what they would like to be different, and (3) the good items should outnumber the "not-so-good" items. If either person uses this as an opportunity to criticize or "dump on" the other, "the week in review" will not work. The other person understandably would not even want to show up for the meeting. (While this exercise was originally designed for use by couples, it is equally useful with your children, other family members, friends, colleagues, etc.).

49.

Tolerance requires that you search for enemies

"In the practice of tolerance, one's enemy is the best teacher."
H. H. the Dalai Lama

What does it say that to practice tolerance, it is best to find an enemy? Is it not better that we see others as our brothers and sisters, rather than adversaries or enemies, so that we do not mistakenly believe that tolerance is necessary? Brothers and sisters can still have disagreements and conflict, but need not view each other as enemies. Instead we can hold out hope for reconciliation and connection. Would this not be better than holding onto fear, resentment and defensiveness?

The Dalai Lama is right. Tolerance prevents me from seeing you as anything other than an enemy. But once I let go of my hatred and allow myself to view you as a potential friend, I can more easily practice understanding, acceptance, even appreciation. I can choose not to be driven by fear.

50.

Tolerance is a bad case of anger management

"All hate is self hate"

A.S. Neill

Founder, Summerhill School

If you get angry it is because of what you think others have done to you; but if you hate it is because of whom you think they are. Anger management teaches you not to hurt someone when you are angry; tolerance teaches you not to hurt someone when you hate them. Both imply that the underlying feeling is justified and to be expected. Neither asks you to examine why it is that you are angry or hateful. And both blame the victim by suggesting that they have done something to anger you or are someone who deserves to be hated. There are far better and more constructive approaches to addressing our differences with the people in our lives. In our classes on nonviolence, we ask the group members to tell us what we mean when we say that

"Behind every angry face is a fearful heart."

By the end of the discussion, some of them are able to see how their anger and hate say more about themselves than about the other person. Anger and hate are more about our own fears, doubts and insecurities than they are about other people's transgressions. Having arrived at that insight, their need for anger management techniques or tolerance strategies decreased dramatically.

Unforgiveable is a made-for-TV movie, based on a true story about Paul and Judy Hegstrom. According to the movie, Paul was abusive toward his wife Judy throughout their 15-year marriage. He then left the family and completed an "anger management" program. After graduation from the program, he and Judy met in a local park at Paul's invitation. During that meeting, Judy expressed her anger at Paul's treatment of her during the marriage.

After that meeting, Paul contacted his anger management counselor to discuss the day's events. Paul reported that even though he didn't hit Judy, he was so mad at what she was saying and doing that he *"wanted to smash her face to get her to stop."* What was the counselor's reaction? *"That's not nothing, Paul, that's everything* (i.e., walking away rather than hitting her). *You did it!"* The counselor did not mention that Paul's desire *"to smash her face to get her to stop"* was an expression of his desire to control Judy and a risk factor for future violence. He apparently was concerned only with whether his client was violent today. As is typical in anger management programs, the underlying feelings and beliefs went unchallenged. Why you are angry does not matter as long as you are not violent. Why you hate a particular group of people does not matter as long as you are tolerant.

51.

Tolerance is the skill of delayed gratification

When our daughter, Emma, was a preschooler, she would often ask during dinner, *"How many bites do I have to eat before I can be done and have dessert?"* Among other lessons, she was learning about delayed gratification. While she learned to "tolerate" longer and longer waiting periods, it was clear that she rarely (if ever) lost sight of her ultimate goal, dessert. So it is with disapproval or hatred. While tolerance requires that you delay expressing your hostility, it does nothing to encourage you to reconsider your hostile attitudes or the inflated sense of entitlement and privilege that often fuels that hostility. Our daughter never said, *"Now that I have had to wait so long for dessert, I guess I don't really want it after all."* If only we could have heard that just once!

52.

Tolerance is never the best option

Tolerance might be worth promoting if the only alternative were intolerance, just as being passive might be a good idea if the only alternative were to be aggressive. Fortunately, neither premise is true.

There are three types of situations – good, bad and neutral. Tolerance is appropriate for none of them. Let's consider them in order. It makes no sense for me to have to tolerate good things (e.g., eating mint chocolate chip ice cream, playing with my cats, spending quality time with my family or reading a good book) because I am too busy appreciating them. Tolerance is clearly not needed.

Second, I shouldn't have to tolerate bad things. For example, you would not tell a victim of child sexual assault that she should just learn to tolerate Uncle Fred. Instead, you would reassure her that she should never have to tolerate the abuse. We would then hold Uncle Fred accountable for his abuse and take whatever steps were necessary to make sure that neither she nor any other child was ever subjected to Fred's abuse again.

Finally, I do not have to tolerate things that are either neutral or irrelevant. For example, I do not have to tolerate even the most inclement weather on top of Mount Washington, as long as I am not on top of that mountain. I might be concerned for someone who is on top of the mountain during a blizzard, but I do not need to tolerate it myself.

So if tolerance makes no sense for the good things in life, should not be imposed for the truly harmful events, and is not needed for the neutral or irrelevant circumstances, then when is it appropriate? Probably never. Perhaps the only good tolerance then, is zero tolerance.

VI.

Religious tolerance

Though the promotion of tolerance in the United States did not become evident until the outlawing of segregation in the late 20th century, it is not a new concept. To fully understand the meaning and impact of tolerance, we must go back to its roots in religion.

Religious tolerance was practiced as long ago as the Roman Empire. When the Romans decided which other religions to tolerate, it was not with the goal of equal regard or power sharing. Clearly, the Romans were in control as the privileged class and could withdraw their tolerance at any time they saw fit. Tolerance did nothing to challenge their inflated sense of privilege or entitlement.

In this chapter, we will discuss other areas within religion where tolerance presents itself.

53.

Many paths, one destination

Eighth grade: it was the year before confirmation. My Presbyterian Sunday school provided us with a unique, eye-opening opportunity. During that year we studied approximately 15 different faiths and visited their services. Services we attended included those for Catholics, Jews, Muslims, Christian Scientists, Mormons, Baptists, Quakers, Buddhists, Hindus, Lutherans and a few others. One week we would learn about some basic tenets of the faith that we were going to visit; the next week we would attend their service. What stood out for me most was how each week I discovered something I liked about this new (to me) faith. For some reason, I never felt that my beliefs were threatened by these "other" religions. Instead, I felt that my religious and spiritual life was enriched by these alternate stories. From this experience, the concept of "religious tolerance" would have been nothing more than a series of nonsense syllables, for I felt no need to defend my religious beliefs from another. There was nothing I needed to tolerate, but plenty that I enjoyed experiencing.

The result is that I often see religions as so many books on one's shelf. You might have a favorite book, but the existence and value of that book is not threatened by the presence of other books on your shelf. You need not feel disloyal when you read and enjoy another one. Nor does your book lose value or authenticity if your neighbor does not choose to own or even read it.

Exercise 12: Celebrating diversity

Purpose: To reduce fear of the unknown by encouraging members of different groups to connect with each other. To help each of us discover our shared humanity and enjoy each other's unique contributions.

Spend a day celebrating another faith or religion. Visit a church or religious service. Without debate or criticism, ask a member of the congregation or their church leader what it is that most defines their faith, what it is that they find most nurturing or sustaining. At mealtime or bedtime recite one of their prayers. Follow one of their customs for the day. For example, if you are a Christian woman and choose to experience Islam for a day, you might want to wear the hijab when you attend a service. Prepare a customary meal. Read about their religion. If you are a teacher, take your class along with you. If you are a parent, involve your children. Think of other ways to experience their faith. At the end of the day, reflect on the experience. Discuss it with others. Was it what you expected? Did you have any fears or concerns prior to this experience? Has the experience changed you or your life? If someone asked you if you were able to be tolerant of this other faith, how would you respond?

Variation: You might also want to try this exercise to develop appreciation for groups based on differences other than religious affiliation (e.g., race, nationality, gender).

54.

Religious acceptance or religious tolerance?

An example of the commonality of religious principles can be found within Unitarian Universalism. According to the organization's website (www.uua.org), Unitarian Universalists include people who identify as Hindus, Pagans, Christians, Muslims, Jews, Atheists, Agnostics and others. Despite the diversity of beliefs that each brings with them, there is a common set of "seven principles that Unitarian Universalist congregations affirm and promote." As stated on their website, these principles include:

"*The inherent worth and dignity of every person;*

Justice, equity and compassion in human relations;

Acceptance of one another and encouragement to spiritual growth in our congregations;

A free and responsible search for truth and meaning;

The right of conscience and the use of the democratic process within our congregations and in society at large;

The goal of world community with peace, liberty and justice for all; [and]

Respect for the interdependent web of all existence of which we are a part."

While it comes as no surprise that mutual acceptance and respect are on the list, it is also noteworthy that religious tolerance is not.

Exercise 13: Christ the Savior?

Purpose: To consider the possibility that markedly different beliefs are complementary, not contradictory, thereby lessening the need for someone to be "tolerant" of another's faith.

How would a Christian, Jew and Muslim each answer the following question: "Is Jesus Christ the Savior of mankind?"

In what way(s) is each of them right? Can all three be right? Why or why not?

What do your answers to these questions tell you about the difference between religious tolerance and religious acceptance?

55.

The ethic of reciprocity

"Once you truly accept all things
you will no longer have to "tolerate" anything."

Charles Cromer, Founder, the Taoist Circle Organization

If there is one universal belief on how we should treat each other it is probably what the Christians refer to as the Golden Rule. In our study, we asked participants what they would *most* like to get from others and what they would *least* like to get from others. As you can see below, tolerance was what they least wanted. So doing unto others as we would have them do unto us, leads us away from tolerance and toward love, understanding, acceptance, respect. For whose benefit are we promoting tolerance?

"What would you ***most*** like to get from others?"

Respect	38%
Acceptance	21%
Understanding	19%
Trust	14%
Appreciation	7%
Tolerance	1%

"What would you ***least*** like to get from others?

Tolerance	72%
Understanding	8%
Acceptance	8%
Appreciation	7%
Respect	3%
Trust	2%

Exercise 14: Personal preference

Purpose: To invite self reflection regarding interpersonal values so that we can determine the importance of tolerance (and other concepts) in our lives.

What would you like to get most from the people in your life (if you could only choose one from the list above)? What would you least like to get? Why? Ask your friends, family, classmates or colleagues what they would most and least want? Do their answers surprise you?

56.

An "eye for an eye"

When we view others as adversaries or enemies, the world becomes unsafe, a potential battleground. We are more likely to think in terms of revenge and retaliation than reconciliation and cooperation. Consider for example the phrase "An eye for an eye." A common interpretation is that *"If you do something bad to me, then I am entitled to do something bad to you."* This interpretation solves nothing, as it only spreads violence, destruction and ill will. As Gandhi famously said,

"An eye for an eye only leaves the whole world blind."

But there is another, equally plausible, and far more constructive interpretation of "An eye for an eye." *"If I take your book, I need to return it. If I break your coffee cup, I need to replace it. If I injure you, I need to compensate you for the damage I caused."* An eye for an eye. This interpretation does not view others as enemies. It does not even focus on the actions of others. It is an example of restorative justice, focusing on personal responsibility. *"How can I be a valued member of the human community, not seen by others as their enemy, but as their friend or neighbor, responsible for my own actions?"*

As a species, our happiness, even our very survival, depends on moving beyond viewing others as enemies. We need to stop asking ourselves whether or not we are capable of tolerating those who are different from us. We need to start recognizing our shared humanity and celebrating our colorful differences.

57.
A Common Word

"Islam teaches tolerance, not hatred; universal brotherhood, not enmity; peace, and not violence."

General Pervez Musharraf
Former President of Pakistan

This statement makes it sound as though tolerance and hatred are inconsistent. Participants in our study felt differently. They believed that tolerance was a component of hatred and violence, rather than an alternative to them. Given that, perhaps it is better to say:

"Islam, by teaching neither hatred, violence nor enmity, has no need for tolerance. Instead, it promotes universal brotherhood and peace."

This rewording is supported by the text of *"A Common Word Between You and Us"* (a letter drafted by Islamic scholars that addressed how the commonalities among Islam, Christianity, and Judaism can form a foundation for universal peace). In this 2007 Open Letter, winner of the 2008 Eugen Biser Award, *"A Common Word"* discusses the scriptural foundation for our common welfare. It makes plentiful references to love, peace, understanding, strength, justice, freedom, etc. as essential values that we all should share. Nowhere, however, does it mention that tolerance is an essential or even peripheral value that we should embrace.

58.
Religious extremism

Since perpetrators attempt to justify their violence based on group differences such as race, color, gender, ability and sexual orientation, why should religion be exempt? Many wars are waged in the name of religion despite theologians' claims that religious doctrines do not endorse killing members of your own species. In one of its most extreme forms, religious violence is referred to as terrorism (i.e., the threat or actual use of violence to terrorize).

How do we reduce or eliminate terrorism? The traditional method is through attacking the so-called terrorists themselves. *Hunt them down and kill them!* One problem is that this method has not proven to be very effective - costly in terms of resources and human life - but not effective. Is there another approach? To explore this, we pose the following question during our classes on nonviolence:

"What is the difference between fighting terrorists and fighting terrorism?"

The discussion usually starts with a distinction. Fighting a terrorist involves attacking a person. In contrast, fighting terrorism involves addressing the motivation for creating fear or terror. If you fight a terrorist, you risk making terrorism worse (because the friends and family of the terrorist will be motivated to seek revenge. Consequently, you create new terrorists, probably more than you eliminated - a counterproductive strategy at best.) But if you fight terrorism, you seek mutual understanding and collaborative problem solving so that the motivation for creating fear and violence is decreased or eliminated. The result is a greater chance for peaceful co-existence. Vastly different strategies based on whether you think people are problems or potential resources to solve problems.

If you attack my enemy, you are a hero. If you attack my friend, you are a terrorist. The difference between a hero and a terrorist is not necessarily what you do, but to whom it is done.

VII.

Equality

"Fourscore and seven years ago our fathers brought forth on this continent, a new nation, conceived in Liberty, and dedicated to the proposition that all men are created equal."
President Abraham Lincoln

Before we discuss the relationship between equality and tolerance, there is an important distinction to be made – the difference between being equal and being identical. Being equal does not mean that you are the same as someone else. Obviously we all have different abilities, interests, talents, beliefs and priorities. There will always be people who perform certain tasks better or worse than we do. When Thomas Jefferson wrote in the Declaration of Independence that we were all created equal, he was well aware of those individual and group differences.

What he was referring to was the importance of recognizing that all people are equally deserving of basic life necessities, of respect, and of the opportunity to lead a rich and full life. It is this view of equality that we will be addressing throughout this chapter. We will then compare tolerance with acceptance, understanding, appreciation and respect with regard to their ability to help us achieve equality.

59.

How are you inferior to me?

"We tend to idealize tolerance, then wonder why we find ourselves infested by losers and nut cases."

Patrick Nielsen Hayden
Essayist

The hostility in his words is apparent, making it clear that we reserve our experience of tolerance for those people whom we consider inferior to ourselves. As Gandhi once said, *"Tolerance implies a gratuitous assumption of the inferiority of other faiths to one's own."* Notice how if we replaced the word "hatred" for "tolerance" (i.e., *"Hatred implies a gratuitous assumption of the inferiority of other faiths to one's own."*) the logic and meaning of the sentence remain intact, suggesting that tolerance is a component of, rather than a solution to, hatred. Tolerance is a decision to postpone the expression of your hatred, rather than a decision to let go of your hatred.

60.

Tolerant men "treat" women as equals

"All men are created equal, It is only men themselves who place them-selves above equality."

David Allan Coe
Country musician

For years, in an effort to encourage men to take a stand against men's violence against women, I implored men to *"treat women as equals."* That is far better than viewing women as inferior, right? Well that is what I thought until someone pointed out to me that "treating" someone as an equal implies that I do not really consider them to be equal, but I am willing to treat them *as if they were equal.* For over a decade of presenting at conferences and workshops, I failed to detect my own condescending sexism expressed in that short phrase.

Treating another group *as if* they were equal is exactly the message of tolerance. *"Deep down I know that you are inferior to me, but I am willing to give you more than you deserve. Why am I willing to do this? I do it because I like to see myself as kind, generous and compassionate. It makes me feel good about myself."* This experience highlighted for me the importance of doing our own mental housecleaning. Sexist, racist, homophobic and similar attitudes can be so subtle and deeply rooted, that they are protected from all but the most serious introspection.

If you are ready to do your own mental housecleaning, try the following exercise.

Exercise 15: Mental housecleaning

Purpose: To discover our own harmful attitudes or beliefs that might be causing conflict or discord in our relationships.

Think of at least one (you get extra credit if you can think of more than one) attitude or belief you harbor that suggests that someone who is different from you is in some way inferior or less deserving. The difference can be racial, religious, cultural, or based on sexual orientation, age, ability, sex, or other characteristic.

Is your belief that they are inferior or less deserving based on fact or is it evidence of an oppressive attitude or prejudice? Can it be both?

If you gave up your belief that they are inferior or less deserving, would it make your life better or worse? In what ways?

61.

Presidential trivia – who was the first to speak out against tolerance?

You might guess that since the abolition of slavery led to segregation and the outlawing of (school) segregation in 1954 led to the promotion of tolerance, that it must have been a fairly recent president who was the first to spot the inherent inequity. You would be wrong.

Ask law professor, Alan Dershowitz, who was quoted in "Affirming diversity: Moving from tolerance to acceptance and beyond" in 2001. According to Professor Dershowitz, it was none other than George Washington.

"Our first president, George Washington, wrote to the tiny Jewish community in Rhode Island that in this new nation, we will no longer speak of mere "toleration," because toleration implies that minorities enjoy their inherent rights "by the indulgence" of the majority."

Even then, we knew that tolerance held no promise of equality.

62.
Don't ask, don't tell

"Tolerance is not ready for equality."
Dale Carpenter
Earl R. Larson Professor of Civil Rights and Civil Liberties Law
University of Minnesota

This "tolerant" military policy regards sexual orientation. *"We won't ask you to disclose your homosexuality. In return we expect you not to tell anyone that you are a homosexual. Under those conditions, we (i.e., heterosexuals in charge) will allow you to serve in our military."* This example of tolerance makes it clear that one group (the tolerant ones) is clearly in the position of power, while the group being tolerated is relatively powerless. Equality is absent when the less powerful group is granted only conditional membership and when the conditions of that membership are determined by the group in power. Consider the following quotation from a former United States Senator from Pennsylvania:

"I have no problem with homosexuality,
I have a problem with homosexual acts."
Rick Santorum, April 7, 2003

That statement makes about as much sense as this one addressing food preferences.

"I have no problem with carnivores as long as they don't eat meat."

Not much point in being a carnivore, if you are not allowed to eat meat. Similarly, there is not much point in being accepted as a homosexual if you are prohibited from engaging in a same-sex relationship.

The homophobic statements in this section are reflective of the problems facing "tolerant" people. They attempt to hide their desire to control or exclude people they disapprove of. Those efforts, however, are not completely successful. Hostility has a way of finding expression, despite its host's best efforts at concealment. The results, in the case of homophobia, are oppressive policies such as "Don't Ask, Don't Tell" and ridiculous statements such as the one made by Mr. Santorum.

Exercise 16: Sexual orientation vs. sexual boundaries

Purpose: To practice detecting logical fallacies that serve to demonize people who, despite being different from us, pose no real threat.

Critique the following statement from a debate on the link between homosexuality and sexual abuse: "Priests who molest boys do so because of a dangerous mix of homosexuality and celibacy. Therefore, the way to protect those children is to either fix the sexual orientation of those men or bar homosexuals from the priesthood."

Do you agree with the above argument? Why or why not?

What assumptions does that argument make about the connection between sexual orientation and sexual offending?

If the above argument were valid, then following the same logic, what policy would we need to implement to protect girls from male priests who attempt to molest them?

How could the above argument be used as a form of tolerant oppression?

63.

All men are created equal

"I never doubted that equal rights was the right direction. Most reforms, most problems are complicated. But to me there is nothing complicated about ordinary equality."

Alice Paul
Suffragist and drafter of the Equal Rights Amendment

The Declaration of Independence demands more than tolerance. *"All men are created equal."* Imagine if Thomas Jefferson had written the following instead: *"We hold these truths to be self evident, that all men deserve to be tolerated, no matter how inferior others judge them to be."* Not quite as compelling, is it?

At least as far back as 1776, we knew that the American Dream did not center on the promotion of tolerance. But the author of that quotation was expressing the views of a people who were fighting against oppression. Prior to the revolution, Americans were not in power. It is important to note that oppressed people are not asking for tolerance. Yet those in power (especially if they want to stay in power) are so generous as to offer it.

Of course, we can do even better than acknowledge that all men are created equal. We can amend that statement to read "All men *and women* are created equal." In rebuttal, some will say that "men" is meant to include women as well, so there is no need to change the wording. How would they react, though, if it were reversed? What if we just said that *"All women are created equal,"* arguing that "women" is meant to include men as well (in fact, the word "women" literally does include as its last three letters, the word "men"). Not many men would feel included if it were reversed that way. Perhaps this is one of the reasons we still have not ratified the Equal Rights Amendment that Alice Paul drafted in 1923.

Exercise 17: Equal rights

Purpose: To examine the reason for our society's, and perhaps personal, reluctance to eradicate sexism, misogyny and gender inequality.

Do you think the ERA should be ratified? Why or why not? What about CEDAW – the Convention on the Elimination of All Forms of Discrimination Against Women (A U.N. Convention)? More than 180 countries have ratified it (but not the U.S.). Why do you think the U.S. has not signed on? Do you think it should?

64.

Tolerance protects people in power

Tolerance protects people in power through strategic planning. By temporarily suspending plans to attack the targets of their tolerance, they can avoid public scrutiny and hold onto their power advantage and inflated sense of entitlement and privilege. As an example, batterers are often mistakenly believed to be frequently or usually violent. The reality though is that violence is usually their tactic of last resort. Why? In contrast to other more subtle forms of control, physical violence leaves evidence that can lead to their apprehension. Once the system gets involved, the batterer's ability to control the victim is compromised. Consequently, the smart batterer uses violence sparingly, strategically, often feeling that he must spend considerable time "tolerating" his victim's behavior. During this period he resorts to a wide range of less obvious forms of abuse, manipulation and control so as to avoid detection. Only when he feels he can no longer put up with what he interprets as her inexcusable disobedience, does he strike out in more obvious ways.

65.

Tolerant oppression within our drug laws

Some forms of oppression are direct, obvious and violent. Tolerant oppression, however, is more subtle. For example, rather than physically attacking homosexual men (which would have been a crime), the dominant culture passed sodomy laws (converting those men's sexual behavior into crimes instead). A similar strategy is used to lock women into prostitution. By making it a crime to be prostituted, those women are unlikely to seek help even when they are raped or beaten by pimps and johns, since doing so might result in their being arrested for engaging in prostitution. Nowhere is this form of tolerant oppression (i.e., criminalizing the behavior of groups you disapprove of) more evident than with our drug laws.

Alcohol, which we erroneously don't even refer to as a drug (as implied by the phrase "alcohol *and* drugs"), has destroyed, even ended, millions of lives through drunk-driving accidents, medical devastation, alcohol poisoning, abrupt withdrawal, and through its connection to violence. At the same time, marijuana has never led to a death due to overdose or withdrawal and the worst risk of aggression while under its influence is probably an unabated attack upon a bag of Doritos. And yet, alcohol is legal, while marijuana is not. Part of the reason for this discrepancy is that the dominant culture sought to control groups of people it did not like but couldn't arrest people for belonging to a different race, culture or other group. So it criminalized the drugs these other cultures preferred (e.g., marijuana, LSD, etc.) while decriminalizing its own drug of choice (i.e., alcohol).

Exercise 18: Removing oppression from the war on drugs

Purpose: To use awareness of oppression to help solve a significant health problem.

Imagine for a moment that we removed from our drug laws any element of oppression so that all drugs and therefore drug users (including alcoholics, heroin addicts, pot smokers, etc.) would be treated equally. What do you suppose would happen if we adopted the same strategy for all drugs that we currently use for alcohol? Specifically, possession and use by adults would be legal as long as the user did not hurt other people or place them in immediate danger. For example, distributing to minors and impaired driving (both of which endanger other people) would be criminal, but personal use or possession would not. Discuss with classmates, colleagues, friends or family, the following questions:

How much money could the system save if non-violent drug users were not arrested, prosecuted or incarcerated and those who were currently incarcerated were released? (Hint: In many correctional facilities, incarceration of a single inmate for a year can cost the taxpayers – yes, you and me – $30,000 to $40,000. So when we say that the defendant should go to jail to "pay for his crime," that is only partially true. We also are paying for his crime.)

Given your answer to the previous question, how much redirected money would now be available for preventive education and affordable or cost-free treatment for those who had a substance abuse problem?

How many current drug addicts who are reluctant to come forward for fear of criminal sanctions, would seek treatment if their behavior was no longer criminalized or demonized and if that treatment were readily available and affordable?

What impact would this new set of non-oppressive policies have on drug-related violence, taking into account the fact that much of drug-related violence is connected to the drugs' illegality, rather than to the psychoactive properties of the drug itself? In answering this question consider the following example: A number of years ago there was such a shortage of cigarettes in parts of Europe that they became black-market items. Coincidentally, reports surfaced of violent attacks perpetrated by cigarette smokers who were trying to access a scarce supply of cigarettes. Does that situation suggest that nicotine should be reclassified as a violent drug? If not, what conclusion do you draw about nicotine-related violence?

(Bear in mind that just because this policy would legalize drug use, it would not necessarily legalize the behavior of the person while using the drug. So if someone refused treatment for a

drug problem and committed an act of violence while intoxicated, the system would come down hard on that person. But the system would respond to the violence, not the drug use per se.)

66.

Tolerance emanates from a superiority complex

"To live anywhere in the world today and be against equality because of race or color is like living in Alaska and being against snow."

William Faulkner
American author

"John thinks he is superior to Bill." The majority of respondents in our study thought that tolerance was consistent with this supremacist attitude. In fact, more respondents connected superiority to tolerance (55%) than to all the other concepts (i.e., acceptance, respect, understanding, trust and appreciation) combined (45%). Tolerance not only fails to guarantee equality, it precludes it.

Consider these reflections on how tolerance makes the people offering it feel better about themselves, without necessarily offering anything of value to those being tolerated:

"No man has a right in America to treat any other man "tolerantly" for tolerance is the assumption of superiority. Our liberties are equal rights of every citizen."

Wendell L. Willkie
Republican nominee for president, 1940

"Britons seem to have given up on assimilating their Muslim population, with many British elites patting themselves on the back for their tolerance and multiculturalism."

Linda Chavez
American author and Chair of the Center for Equal Opportunity

"Good breeding consists in concealing how much we think of ourselves and how little we think of the other person."

Mark Twain
American author

Tolerance (as opposed to intolerance) is very much about concealment. And if your "breeding" was good enough to hide how you feel
about yourself in relation to others, you will be acknowledged for your
effort and "sacrifice," as indicated by statements from Frank Knox,
publisher of the Chicago Daily News (*"I believe with all my heart that
civilization has produced nothing finer than a man or woman who thinks and
practices true tolerance."*) and Helen Keller (*"The highest result of education
is tolerance."*) The question for me then is, do I want to impress people
with how privileged or well educated I am, or do I want to find a way
to relate to them as equals?

67.
Disabilities

"Much too little to tolerate the difference,
because tolerance evokes superiority."

Franca Eckert Coen
Advisor to the Mayor of Rome

Nowhere is the belief of inequality more evident than with the concept of disabilities. Not only do people look down on those with disabilities, but the inequity is expressed in the term itself. *"You are disabled, I am not. Therefore, I am better than you."* But the fact is, we all have abilities and disabilities, things we are good at and things with which we need assistance from others. Some people who have the most significant disabilities, also demonstrate the greatest genius.

The truth is that we are all differently "abled" and differently challenged. If we were to accept others for who they are (rather than "tolerate" those who are different from us) would not the experience of those we currently refer to as having documented disabilities, improve? Would not all of us benefit by discovering the treasure of talents we all have to share?

Exercise 19: Disabilities

Purpose: To challenge prejudicial attitudes toward, and discrimination against, those with disabilities by examining underlying attitudes.

Do you know anyone who does everything better than you do?

Do you know anyone who does everything worse than you do?

How many people do you know personally who have documented disabilities?

What is each of their greatest abilities?

*What is the difference between a disabled person and a person with disabilities?

*Pick a condition that is often referred to as a disability (e.g., autism, epilepsy, paraplegia). Using the internet or other resources, find at least five famously talented people who share that condition.

*After thinking about, researching and answering these questions, what did you learn about disabilities, and your attitudes toward people with disabilities?

68.

Looking down on people who are better than you?

"In America everybody is of the opinion that he has no social superiors, since all men are equal, but he does not admit that he has no social inferiors, for, from the time of Jefferson onward, the doctrine that all men are equal applies only upwards, not downwards."

Bertrand Russell
Mathematician and philosopher

Some might say that tolerance is not always about condescension because we might tolerate people who are smarter or more talented than we are. You cannot look down at someone who is above you, right? Actually you can. The reason is that it is not their genius or talent that we say we resent, it is the way they rub it in our faces, the way they annoy us, the way they show off, etc. The unspoken message is *"Those people are annoying while I am not, so my lack of annoyance is what makes me superior to them."*

You might counter by saying that my belief that I am superior simply because I am allegedly less annoying is really a distortion of reality. And you would be right. But that is the nature of tolerance. It is ALWAYS a distortion of reality. Tolerance assumes that one person is superior to another. Tolerance seems to ignore the truth that our founding fathers believed to be self evident – that all of us are created equal.

69.

Comments from study participants

"I don't want charity, I want equality."
"What makes them think they are so much better than us?"
"What happened to 'All men are created equal.'?"
"I'm tired of that 'holier than thou' crap."
"It just widens the gap between the haves and the have not's."
"Tolerance? How condescending!"
"Isn't that what supremacists do?"
"A survival strategy for supremacists."
"Internalized racism"
"Tolerance is a quiet racial slur."

Study participants

70.

Promoting equality through cooperation and power sharing

Segregation does not just involve sending children with different racial or cultural identities to separate schools. It also occurs within schools based on academic abilities. Children are often divided into tracks (e.g., "gifted," "mainstream," "learning disabled." The terms themselves have misleading, divisive and destructive effects on classmates.). The rationale for such separation can be gleaned from the following comments from parents. *"My daughter is really bright. Those other students will just slow her down." "My child needs extra attention. He'll get lost when he can't keep up with the other kids in his class."* These are understandable concerns that need to be addressed.

In some schools, however, children of varying abilities are deliberately placed in the same classroom, in part to address the concerns listed above. Here is how it has worked in some districts. The children who have the easiest time learning certain material are enlisted as teacher's aides. Instead of getting bored, they end up learning the material even better than before, because now they have to know it well enough to teach it. The students who experience the greatest difficulty learning that material benefit because they now have additional tutors in the classroom. All of the students benefit from the increased social interactions of this cooperative (rather than competitive) learning environment.

In addition, while some students are good in math, others might be good in reading, while still others are good in art or music. No one is good or bad at everything. So the teacher's aides shift from topic to topic. This helps children to learn a vital lesson. It is not how smart you are that is important. Instead, it is how you are smart. We all have areas of relative strength and weakness. An important question then is *"How do we use our strengths and abilities? Do we use them to make our lives and the lives of those around us better or do we use them to exploit and dominate?"*

Exercise 20: Promoting equality not tolerance

Purpose: To identify real and tangible benefits that oppressors would enjoy by giving up their abusive dominance and sharing power.

It is relatively easy to think of ways that oppression harms those who are subject to discrimination and prejudice. In this exercise, you are invited to think of ways that oppression harms or limits the oppressor. Punishing oppressors or just telling them to be more tolerant will only lead to greater resentment. We must be able to articulate the clear benefits (and there are many) of giving up oppression through the sharing of power.

In your culture, who is the oppressor and who is the target of that oppression in each of the following? How can the last one, "rankism" be seen as including all the others?

Sexism

Racism

Heterosexism

Classism

Ableism

Religism

Ageism

Nationalism

Rankism

What does the oppressor gain through holding these people down?

What would the oppressor gain by giving up dominance and sharing power instead? (For example, in most cultures, men are in a position of power over women. One way that those men benefit from sexism is by earning more money than women for the same job. On the other hand, if they shared power equally, they would experience less stress from believing that they need to be the sole provider). See if you can identify other benefits and costs associated with sexism for men. Then do the same with the other forms of oppression listed above. What other forms of oppression would you add to the list?

71.

Then segregation, now tolerance

"Those who cannot remember the past are condemned to repeat it."

George Santayana
American (Spanish-born) philosopher

The inability to detect social inequities is not limited to the average citizen. Such insensitivity has reached as high as the U.S. Supreme Court. For example, in 1896, the U.S. Supreme Court constitutionally sanctioned the "Separate but Equal" doctrine in the Plessy v. Ferguson case. Justice Brown wrote on behalf of the court that if Blacks felt that *"forced separation"* stamped them with *"a badge of inferiority"* it had nothing to do with the legislation itself but instead was *"solely because the colored race chooses to put that construction upon it."* Only one justice, John Marshall Harlan, (the single dissenting vote in a 7-1 decision) detected the supremacist attitude. He said that the Louisiana law created a *"badge of servitude"* that degraded Black Americans. He also correctly predicted that this law would become as infamous as the Dred Scott decision, which in large part denied U.S. citizenship to both those who had been enslaved and their descendants, even if they were born in the U.S.

Now fast forward to the 21st century. We are being told by some civic and religious leaders that if we are offended by the promotion of tolerance, it is not because there is anything intrinsically wrong with the concept, but it is only because we are misunderstanding what the word really means. Sound familiar?

72.

Eracism

"The removal from existence the belief
that one race is superior to another."
Definition of Eracism found on a t-shirt

In January of 2006, Lou Gosssett, Jr. founded a non-profit organization, The Eracism Foundation, Inc. whose mission is *"to eradicate the systematic impacts of all forms of racism by providing programs that foster cultural diversity, historical enrichment, education, and antiviolence initiatives."* It should come as no surprise by now that the eraser with which we are to remove racism was not intended to leave the stain of tolerance.

73.
Throw a tolerance party

Go ahead and celebrate your tolerant attitudes. Invite people your group has oppressed over the years and tell them you just want to show them how much you've come to tolerate them. Hold a tolerance parade. Reassure those in attendance – *"Know that you are tolerated by one and all!"* Are you a member of a dominant religion? Let's say you are Christian in a largely Christian community. Try handing out buttons to your Jewish, Muslim, or Buddhist neighbors that read *"I was tolerated by a Christian today."* Ask them to wear that button home, or to work. See what they say. Take a poll. Start a petition asking people to register their commitment to tolerate minorities. Let the whole world know that you are the kind of person who is willing to tolerate people who appear to be different from you.

If you truly believe that tolerance is wonderful or essential, you should not hesitate to do any of these.

Exercise 21: Lift up and help down

Purpose: To apply the notion that "change occurs one person at a time" to the achievement of equality.

No matter who you are or what groups you belong to, there are people with more power than you and people with less. This discrepancy in power contributes to so many social ills. We are in need of an adjustment, much like the type a chiropractor would perform on a misaligned spine. Each of us is in a position to help with that realignment.

One way to do this is to identify one person you know who abuses power and another who is being disempowered, and then reach out to both. What is it that the person in power fears? What stands in his way of sharing power? Why does he feel a need to push others down? Help him to see that sharing power will help his fear to go away and improve his life. Perhaps it is a heterosexual who is afraid to share the institution of marriage with non-hetero-sexuals. Help him to see that his marriage is not in jeopardy if two

*men or women marry each other. Reassure him that homosexual-
ity is not contagious, anymore than heterosexuality is.*

*Reach out to someone who is being oppressed. Perhaps a fel-
low student is bullying him at school. Stand beside him and inform
the bully that such abuse will not be tolerated; that your friend is as
deserving of respect as anyone else, even the bully. Once you have
"lifted up" someone who is being oppressed and "helped down"
someone who is abusing his power, invite others to do the same. If
each of us makes these small adjustments in our families, neigh-
borhoods and communities, we can approach the equality that
makes every healthy society thrive.*

74.

Deviation from a norm

"The allowable deviation from a standard"
Dictionary definition of tolerance

When someone radically deviates from a norm, we might call that person a "deviant." It is a pejorative label, and appropriately so if for example their deviance involves having sex with farm animals. Not every deviation, though, is negative. Geniuses such as Einstein or elite athletes such as Roger Federer also radically deviate from a norm, but in a good way. I have never heard anyone refer to them as deviants, though statistically speaking, they qualify.

The problem with the concept of deviancy is that its pejorative connotations serve to equate "different" with "bad." Therefore, anyone who does not conform to a common standard, practice or belief might be viewed as a threat, a threat that society must then decide whether or not to tolerate. If we did not assume that deviation from a norm was automatically a problem, then tolerance would less likely be a consideration.

Take for example, the 2003 Supreme Court case, Lawrence v. Texas. In this case, law enforcement officers responded to a false tip regarding a disturbance in an apartment. When the officers entered the apartment, they found two men engaged in homosexual activity. The men were arrested for, and convicted of, engaging in "deviate sexual intercourse." Even though their conviction was upheld by the Appeals Court, the U.S. Supreme Court overturned the conviction on both privacy and equal protection grounds. Justice Kennedy's majority opinion, (a six to three decision), stated that consenting adults have a right to engage in sexual activities regardless of whether their behavior statistically deviates from the norm. Prior to this decision, it was up to the states to determine which consensual activities to tolerate (i.e., which ones were "allowable deviations from the norm" and which were not). The decision in Lawrence v. Texas rendered the consideration of tolerance legally irrelevant. It is no longer permissible (on constitutional grounds) for the dominant culture to pass judgment on and restrict consensual sexual activity simply because they disapprove of it.

75.

Baseball's perfect game

*"I'm not concerned with your liking or disliking me...
All I ask is that you respect me as a human being."*

Jackie Robinson
Baseball player

In baseball, a perfect game refers to one in which the winning team does not allow even one player from the opposing team to reach first base. No runs, ho hits, no walks, nothing. Twenty-seven up, twenty-seven down. While this is considered a perfect success for the winning team, it is perfect humiliation for the other. Total ineffectiveness. Complete failure. To call this a perfect game only considers the experience of half of the players involved. Let's consider another type of perfect game in baseball. One that considers the outcome for everyone involved.

As far as I know, there has only been one such game played, the 2002 Major League's All Star Game, which had an unexpected and unprecedented outcome. After nine innings of play, the game was tied. Not a problem, you say. Just play extra innings. And so they did, two extra innings to be exact. But by the end of the eleventh inning with the game still tied, there was a problem. The two teams ran out of pitchers. In most games, you would not run out of pitchers from your bullpen so early into extra innings and even if you did, you might ask one of your starting pitchers to come in for a few innings. But in the All Star Game, the managers attempt to give everyone a chance to play, so each pitcher on their roster is only in the game for an inning or two.

Here is what happened. At the end of the eleventh inning, the two managers and the Baseball Commissioner Bud Selig met on the field to discuss their predicament. Each manager explained that he could not ask his current pitcher to throw another inning for two reasons. First, to do so would increase the chance of injury to this "all-star" pitcher, not something that would please his regular team or its fans. Second, the All Star game does not really count for anything. It does not factor into pennant races or have any other impact on the regular season or the playoffs.

Consequently, Commissioner Selig went to the microphone and in as apologetic voice as he could muster, informed the fans that they had decided to just stop the game. *Hope you enjoyed the game. It's time to go home.* The fans' reaction was clear. They were not happy, as evidenced by the loud booing and hissing. Some fans were throwing garbage onto the field. Others cried "Rippoff!!" and chanted "Refund, refund!!!"

Let's take a look at the ways in which these fans were "ripped off." They paid for nine innings of baseball and received ONLY eleven. Hmmm. Last time I checked, eleven was more than nine. Imagine you go into a store to buy nine shirts. You take those shirts to the cash register. The manager, noticing your relatively large purchase, offers to give you two extra shirts at no additional charge, just for being a good customer, eleven for the price of nine. Would you be outraged? Would you accuse the manager of ripping you off and report him to the Better Business Bureau?

Some might say that the real problem was that this game ended before there was a winner. Is that really true? First, just being selected an "All-Star" is a victory of sorts. It is quite an honor for which many players receive financial bonuses from their teams. Second, this is an exhibition game; winning it does nothing to affect the rest of baseball season. Therefore, "winning" has little meaning. Third, prior to this game, the National League had lost five All Star games in a row. The American League therefore had won the last five. At the end of this "tie" game, we actually had two winners. The National League had broken its losing streak and the American League kept its unbeaten streak intact. In an unprecedented fashion, both leagues won. Fourth, in every other baseball game, one team and its fans go home disappointed that their team lost. In this game, no one had to suffer the disappointment of defeat. No fan or player had to go home and admit that his team lost. What could be better than that?

So if the fans enjoyed more innings than they paid for and there were plenty of winners, what was missing? Why were the fans so outraged? The only thing missing was a loser, someone to feel superior to. *I'm not satisfied with my victory unless someone else is suffering because of it.*

So here is what really happened in this game. After eleven innings of baseball between the (arguably) 30 best players from each league, we determined that, at least for this brief moment, the leagues were equal. Neither better than the other. Now that is a perfect game! But this conclusion outraged us. *How dare you suggest that we achieved or demonstrated equality!* We say we want to achieve equality. It is even part of our Declaration of Independence, but when we achieve or demonstrate it, we are not happy. When Commissioner Selig addressed the fans, he apologized profusely for this "unfortunate" outcome and promised to make sure that it would never happen again. (He did that by awarding home field advantage in the World Series to the team representing the league that won the All Star game.)

This is not the first time in baseball that fans were outraged, booed and threw garbage onto the field. The other time was in 1947, when Jackie Robinson broke the color barrier by playing his first game for the Brooklyn Dodgers. Fans were livid. *How dare we suggest that there should be racial equality; that Blacks and Whites should have equal access to major league baseball?*

76.

Competition not equality?

A colleague warned me that the previous section on baseball might alienate sports fans who would say *"When it comes to sports, I'm interested in competition, not equality."* She made a good point, which brought to mind a common assumption – that competition and equality are mutually exclusive. We certainly set up our sporting events as if that were true. When the score is tied at the end of regulation, we employ extra innings, shootouts, tiebreakers, or a game seven "if necessary." Necessary? Why is it necessary to break the tie? What is the worst thing that would happen if we left it even? Co-champions? Mutual victory? Two winners and no losers? Would a sporting event be any less "competitive" if occasionally the athletes performed equally well (in fact, are not those the *most* competitive events. Consider, for example, the first round match of Wimbledon in 2010 between John Isner and Nicolas Mahut. That was a three-day, eleven-hour, five-set match that Isner won by taking the fifth set 70 to 68. It was by far the most competitive tennis match ever played *because* the players performed equally well.)?

Every time a sporting event concludes, we are reminded of our distinctions, what makes us different from (and hopefully better than) another. We even measure how superior one person or team is. *"He won by a record 12 strokes." "Their average margin of victory was 11 points." "He set a world record by more than a second." "That was the worst defeat they have suffered in 10 years."*

For better or worse, professional athletes are role models. Ad slogans such as *"Be like Mike"* (referring to basketball star Michael Jordan) acknowledge the impact of an athlete's or a team's performance on spectators. It seems that sports teach us everything we need to know about defeating people (*"The thrill of victory and the agony of defeat"*). Should it not also teach us (at least occasionally) how to share success with other competitors, and that there are benefits when we do *not* defeat the other person?

Exercise 22: Modeling equality in sports

Purpose: To explore the benefits of mutual victories in sports, especially as a model for promoting equality and sharing success outside the sporting world.

Discuss the following questions:

What is the impact on us when our sports "heroes" demonstrate that there must always be a loser, a distinction between people, one person or group of people better than another?

For example, what effect does it have on our attempts to resolve interpersonal conflict? Instead of ensuring that both "sides" get their needs met, do we strive to win an argument, win a war, or otherwise come out on top? Does peaceful co-existence become less of a realistic outcome?

How does the requirement of hierarchical distinctions in sports reinforce the sense of privilege and entitlement claimed by people who believe that theirs is the only "true" religion, "master" race, "normal" sexual orientation, or "superior" gender?

Imagine that you have just been hired as the new commissioner of a sport and that one of your job responsibilities is to revise the rules so that mutual victories are possible. Other than eliminating tiebreakers how could you support equal outcomes? Would you create a special trophy or shared prize for events that end with multiple winners? If so, after whom would you name that award? Would you encourage the mutual victors to do joint press interviews or talk to high school students about the value of recognizing equality? How else could you market this rare outcome so that it would be celebrated just as we celebrate world records, a 300 in bowling, a grand slam in tennis or golf, or the Triple Crown in horse racing?

77.

The abortion debate

"No one is pro-abortion"

President Barack Obama

If a leading cause of abortion is the oppression of women, then a major strategy for reducing abortion is the empowerment of women.

What would happen to the so-called abortion debate if we abandoned condescending attitudes, including tolerance? What if we refused to view people as the problem and instead viewed them as resources with whom we could solve problems? We probably would not refer to ourselves as pro-life or pro-choice; nor would we refer to others as anti-life or anti-choice. Those labels serve to demonize people who disagree with us and create or reinforce barriers to collaborative problem solving. This strategy is both distracting and nonproductive.

If we were to view people as resources, we might not even think that abortion was the primary concern. We might realize that abortion is only one of many attempted solutions to problems that arise with pregnancies. Sometimes the pregnancies are unintended (e.g., due to failed birth control or a result of rape or incest). Sometimes they are unsupported due to lack of financial, medical or other resources. Sometimes they are highly desired, but a change in circumstances such as medical complications alters the equation. Sometimes it is not the pregnancy that is "problematic" but the culture that fails to support women who need to make reproductive choices.

While there are endless debates about the nature of the "problem" and whether abortion should be legal, there is no disputing that we all would benefit by reducing the problems associated with pregnancies. That would be our common ground. Try this exercise on collaborative problem solving.

Exercise 23: Problems associated with pregnancies

Purpose: To demonstrate how searching for common ground can be an effective tool to empower victims of oppression while addressing specific issues such as problems associated with pregnancies.

See how many strategies you can think of that would reduce the problems associated with pregnancies (and hence reduce the need for abortions) without passing a single law against abortion, without staging a single protest outside an abortion clinic, and without engaging in a single argument about abortion with anyone. Refer to one of the quotations at the beginning of this section: "If a leading cause of abortion is the oppression of women, then a major strategy for reducing abortion is the empowerment of women." Keeping that in mind, how can you effectively reduce the incidence of abortion by empowering, rather than criticizing, restricting, or oppressing women?"

You should be able to come up with several strategies. I'll give you the first one.

Protect women. How many women in your area (city, state or country) are raped each year? How many of them are impregnated by their rapist? Many of these women understandably report problems associated with their pregnancies (at the very least, how someone impregnated them). Protect women from rape and you automatically reduce the number of potential and therefore actual abortions. What about domestic violence during pregnancy? How many batterers physically attack their pregnant partners, intentionally causing them to miscarry? (In my nonviolence classes, I have met several.) These miscarriages are "batterer-induced abortions." Protecting women from domestic and sexual violence is effectively a "pro-life" strategy.

See how many other strategies you can identify. (Hint: The most promising strategies will probably not involve criminal justice sanctions or constitutional amendments. They will more likely involve enlisting resources from the healthcare, education, workplace and similar arenas to support women in their reproductive decision making.) How does each of your strategies demonstrate that being "pro-choice" is effectively "pro-life" as well?

78.

Sexual violence

"In a society in which equality is a fact, not merely a word, words of racial or sexual assault and humiliation will be nonsense syllables. "

Catherine MacKinnon
Elizabeth A. Long Professor of Law
University of Michigan

Early sexualization of children, prostitution and pornography, sexual and street harassment, human trafficking as modern day slavery, incest, the marital rape exemption and war time rape are all forms of sexual violence made possible by viewing human beings as sexual objects, as less than deserving of basic human dignity and civil rights.

Consider the gender inequity in sexuality. Men who are sexually active are often referred to as "the man," "a player," "a stud." A man is often asked if he scored last night, as if sex were an Olympic event. Women on the other hand are penalized for engaging in sexual activity. They are referred to with derogatory terms such as "whore" and "slut." Nowhere is this imbalance more apparent than with prostitution.

Who pays women as much as it takes to get them to be prostitutes?
Men.

Who enacted legislation criminalizing prostitution?
Men.

Who calls those women disgusting names for being prostitutes?
Those same men.

That's interesting. We call women names and arrest them for doing what we pay them to do. That is the hallmark of oppression. Put a group of people down then blame and punish them for being down there.

All countries should do what Sweden does with regard to prostitution. Rather than endorsing condescending attitudes toward women, they realize that prostitution is not a job, but an oppressive institution of sexual exploitation and violence. Consequently, they criminalize prostitution, but not for the women and children (and sometimes men) being prostituted. They criminalize the actions of the pimps, traffickers and johns. They believe that arresting people who have been prostituted is in reality arresting and re-victimizing sexual assault survivors. What has been the impact of Sweden's legislation and cultural awareness? They have achieved impressive results in reducing the rates of prostitution (not just what is considered human trafficking, but all forms of prostitution).

"One of the greatest gifts to our industry [prostitution] was the creation of the anti-trafficking movement. By distinguishing between trafficked victims and other prostitutes, you've legitimized prostitution as a business. Our new motto: "Buy local.""
Self described "pimp."

VIII.

Acceptance

"The time is past for promoting only 'tolerance.' We need to urge and strive for acceptance."
Cheryl Garner Shaw
Former Unity Council Director, Sacramento, CA

"Happiness can only exist in acceptance."
George Orwell
Journalist and essayist

When I ask people who are *offended* by tolerance, what comes to mind when they hear that word, they often say "disapproval." In contrast, when I ask people who *promote* tolerance what comes to mind, they usually say "acceptance." How do we resolve these widely disparate reactions? Is tolerance on the path toward acceptance, or does it move us in the opposite direction toward "unacceptable?" For programs that promote equality, the policy implications are both obvious and significant. If we want people to regard each other as equals, there is no room for "disapproval" in the message. There is plenty of room, however, for "acceptance." This chapter is devoted to exploring that debate.

79.

Tolerance is at best ambiguous

"Tolerance is an ambiguous and complex concept open to several interpretations ranging from forbearance to full acceptance."

From "Love Thy Neighbours:
Racial Tolerance Among Young Australians"

Tolerance is highly offensive to some people, yet highly defended by others. Does it mean full acceptance of differences or does it reflect a condescendingly complete lack of acceptance? It depends on whom you ask. At best it has become ambiguous. But ambiguity is not a reason to use a word; it's a reason to find another. If a word can mean one thing and also the opposite, then at best it is useless. At worst, dangerous.

For example, imagine we coin a word "gzorntenblat." Let's assume it can mean either healthy or unhealthy. We then assert that smoking is gzorntenblat. We either have offered no information about whether smoking is a health risk (because you don't know if we meant healthy or unhealthy) or worse, we make it easier for cigarette manufacturers to avoid responsibility for endangering the welfare of its consumers. *"We warned them"* claimed the cigarette manufacturers. *"We said that smoking was gzorntenblat!"* The same risk applies to the use of the word tolerance.

During the 2008 campaign, when Vice Presidential candidate Sarah Palin claimed that she was tolerant of homosexuals, was she suggesting that she considers them to be inferior, but puts up with them because she has to? Probably. But she could also claim that she meant that she accepts them fully (less likely), because some define tolerance as full acceptance. Let us not make it easier for supremacists to avoid accountability by providing them with a term that lends itself to plausible deniability.

80.

Acceptance is not the same as agreement

Tolerance is what happens when you allow fear to stand between you and acceptance.

Some people are afraid to accept those who are different from them for fear that such acceptance suggests that they are also in agreement. For example, I recall one homophobic man saying:

"If I refuse to make fun of a gay man, my friends will think that I'm gay. Don't ask me to do that. It would ruin my rep[utation]."

He was afraid that his friends would confuse agreement and acceptance. But you can accept people without agreeing with them. Agreement is not something you choose. For example, if people tell me that two plus two equals four, I do not *choose* to agree with them. I just *notice* that I do. In contrast, if people have different religious beliefs than I do, or have different sexual preferences, then my accepting them simply means that I make no effort to judge or control them. My acceptance means that I do not need them to think, feel, perceive or act in the way that I do. Acceptance is a model of peaceful co-existence, a live-and-let-live philosophy. If that acceptance is a struggle for us or if we find ourselves feeling impatient, then we are more likely experiencing tolerance than acceptance.

81.

An American man in India

I am lucky. Through no effort of my own, I am a white, hetero-sexual, male U. S. citizen who is reasonably intelligent and well edu-cated and who has no documented disabilities. It was neither my choice to be part of this dominant culture, nor do I deserve more than those who are less privileged than I. But the advantages are mine to enjoy nonetheless.

So I know little about being oppressed, about what it is like for the dominant culture to decide whether or not to tolerate my existence. The only time I recall experiencing this kind of tolerance was several years ago when I traveled to India to learn about their efforts to address violence against women. One morning I took a train to India Gate in New Delhi to go for a run. When I boarded the train at 6 AM I was dressed in a short sleeve shirt and running shorts, even though the other passengers were wearing coats and long pants. I quickly felt eyes upon me. It could have just been my imagination, but they did not feel like "accepting" eyes (*He sure is different. How interesting our diverse cul-ture can be.*) They were "tolerant" eyes (*You don't fit in. You dress wrong, are too tall, too white, too American. We'll put up with you if we have to, but it would be better if you just left.*) That tolerance felt awful. It made me want to disappear.

When I arrived at my afternoon meeting at *Jagori*, a prominent victim advocacy agency in New Delhi, I shared my experience with the staff. They immediately asked me if there was any point at which I felt unsafe. What a great question! I never doubted my safety, not even for a moment. They suggested that if I were a white woman from the United States in the same circumstances, safety might be my primary concern. It made me realize that while tolerance can cause discomfort for anyone, it is especially problematic for vulnerable populations since tolerance can quickly turn into intolerance when the dominant culture decides to assert its will.

82.

The only good tolerance is zero tolerance

If someone truly harms you, you should not have to tolerate that behavior. But if there is no harm, you have no business tolerating them.

Many communities have enacted "zero tolerance" policies with regard to child abuse, sexual assault, drunk driving and other behaviors that cause direct and devastating harm to the victims. This seems to be an appropriate use of the word tolerance. If you are truly harming another person, your behavior should not be tolerated.

But what if the objectionable behavior does not harm anyone else? For example, you might not like it when other people chew food with their mouths open. If you were a tolerant person, you would still be bothered by their behavior, but you would keep your objections to yourself and put up with their bad table manners. You might point out your objections to a friend of yours, but you would avoid a direct conversation with the person whose behavior you disapprove of. In contrast, people who accept (rather than tolerate) others as they are would have decided that their table manners are none of their business, and would be bothered far less since they would divert their attention to matters that were their business. Perhaps they share Plato's view of justice:

"Justice means minding one's own business and not meddling with other men's concerns."

83.

Making the world a great place to live

To appreciate diversity, acceptance is a precondition, while tolerance is a preclusion.

What would be *most* effective in making the world a great place to live?

Accept each other	34%
Strive to understand	25%
Be respectful	24%
Be tolerant	7%
Show appreciation	5%
Trust each other	5%

What would be *least* effective in making the world a great place to live?

Be tolerant	65%
Strive to understand	11%
Show appreciation	9%
Trust each other	7%
Accept each other	4%
Be respectful	4%

Dr. Martin Luther King, Jr. talked about building a "beloved community." We asked our study participants what they thought would be most and least helpful in building the kind of world they would like to see. According to them, we should focus our energies on encouraging people to accept and understand each other, and be more respectful. In contrast, they overwhelmingly believed that the least successful strategy was to encourage people to be more tolerant.

Exercise 24: Making the world a great place to live

Purpose: To encourage thoughtful comparison of interpersonal values.

Which of the above goals do you think would have the greatest chance of making the world a great place to live (if you could choose only one)? Which do you think would be least effective? Ask your friends, family, classmates or colleagues what they think. Do their answers surprise you?

84.

The serenity prayer

"God give me the serenity to accept the things that I cannot change, the courage to change the things I can and the wisdom to know the difference."

Popular in 12-step programs, the serenity prayer addresses the importance of investing energy in areas that are within your control and letting go of everything else. This is the essence of acceptance. *"You and I might be different but I accept you as you are for two reasons. First, it is none of my business to decide who you should be. Second, it is a far better use of my time to focus on who I should be."* "Tolerant" people do not enjoy such serenity. They can never truly let go of their desire to change other people. For now, they remain silent on the outside, but do not let go on the inside. Their disapproval often continues to grow into resentment until they can take it no longer. Then they finally speak out against the people who are not living up to their standards.

Tolerance is allowing other people to break your rules (at least for now). Acceptance is the belief that it is not up to you to decide what rules other people have to follow.

Years ago, while I was managing a substance abuse clinic, a client told me that as long as he focused on the alcohol that he was trying not to consume, he found no peace, no serenity in his life. Life had become intolerable and unmanageable. But when he shifted his focus to what he could have (rather than what he shouldn't have), he was better able to accept the things that he could not change (e.g., that his relationship to alcohol and other drugs had caused severe problems in his life). He believed that his attempts to tolerate everything that was wrong in his life made his drinking worse. In contrast, letting go of (i.e., accepting) the things he could not change, gave him the strength to regain control over his life.

85.

Stages of grief

Peace does not require happiness. Sometimes it is just a successful journey from tolerance to acceptance.

Dr. Elisabeth Kubler-Ross wrote extensively about the process of grief, especially with dying patients. She described five common stages (denial, anger, bargaining, depression and either acceptance or resignation) that dying patients and their families go through while they grieve their impending loss. When the grieving process is productive and healthy, acceptance is the end goal, suggesting that the person is no longer struggling against reality. Resignation is the unhealthy outcome. In contrast to acceptance, resignation suggests that they have given up, resigning themselves to the realization that they will never be able to accept what they now know to be true. During my five years working on a suicide hotline, resignation was a commonly heard concern. *"I finally realize that nothing will make life bearable and have resigned myself to my fate. I must now end my life."*

Interestingly, sometimes I would hear the language of tolerance within that struggle. *"I just can't tolerate the pain anymore."* Tolerance was never seen as the solution; it was just something they would do until the pain went away or until they realized the pain would never go away and they became actively suicidal. Tolerance was a symptom of how bad life had become, rather than a strategy to make it better. It never seemed to improve life. Instead it was a painful reminder of their misery. I never would have been so insensitive as to suggest to a suicidal person, *"You should just learn to tolerate your circumstances."*

86.

Tolerance quietly passes judgment

> To eliminate de jure segregation, all you need is tolerance; to eliminate de facto segregation, you need acceptance.

Acceptance seems to convey the opposite or absence of judgment. Can the same be said of tolerance? *"John thinks there is definitely something wrong with Bill."* Only 10% of the participants in our study thought acceptance was the best choice (instead, they were more likely to think *"I can accept you, flaws and all"*); thirty-five (35) percent chose understanding (e.g., *"I've got your number,"* and *"I'm on to you!"*). The most judgmental concept though, was tolerance at 54%. How will we be able to create the beloved community that Dr. King had envisioned if we promote such a judgmental concept?

87.

Tolerance leads to rejection, not acceptance

"Tolerance to alcohol is not a step in the right direction — toward the body's acceptance of the toxin; it is a step in the wrong direction, toward death."

Substance abuse counselor

Consider tolerance to alcohol. The more one drinks alcohol, the more tolerance that person develops, so that more needs to be consumed to feel the same intoxicating effects. But the increasing tolerance is not a measure of success or improvement; it is a symptom of the disease, a measurement of the destruction. The more tolerance one acquires, the closer that person is to death. Tolerance is the enemy. The solution is to not drink alcohol, to stay away from the toxin. When you attempt to apply that "solution" to people you tolerate, it is called segregation. So the solution to tolerance is segregation? Or was the solution to segregation, tolerance? What then is the solution or healthy alternative to both? Acceptance? Respect?

88.
Acceptance or tolerance – it's your choice

"Acceptance and coexistence would be much preferable to tolerance as a precondition and as a goal to strive for – the coexistence of partners enjoying equal rights and working together for a better future."

Professor Gerhard Bodendorfer
Institute for Old Testament Biblical Research
Salzburg, Austria

It is possible that what one accepts is negative. But it is always true, that what one tolerates is negative or at least believed to be so. Have you ever heard someone try to justify the use of the word "acceptance" by saying that what they really mean is tolerance? Unlikely. But often, efforts are made to justify the use of tolerance by trying to equate it to acceptance. For example, consider the following statement in defense of tolerance:

"The strongest, and perhaps, most ideal way to think of tolerance depends on full acceptance of others when differences between the 'others' and oneself are recognised."

"Love Thy Neighbours"

If what you mean is "acceptance," why not just say that and avoid the confusion and ambiguity? In a 2004 personal communication addressing the confusion between tolerance and acceptance, Julian Bond (Chairman of the NAACP and former Board Chair of the Southern Poverty Law Center) suggested to me that

"Perhaps more will use "acceptance" instead of tolerance."

Yes, you must choose one or the other. I choose acceptance. Which one will you choose?

89.

Tolerance minus frustration equals acceptance

Tolerance is the itch you are not able to scratch; acceptance is no longer focusing on that sensation.

Frustration is what you feel when you focus on things over which you have no control. The longer you persist, the more frustrated you become. The purpose of our being able to feel frustration is to tell us when our energies are misplaced. Frustration encourages us to shift our focus, change our strategies or do something else altogether. Once we redirect our attention, the frustration goes away. Tolerance, which suggests that you are putting up with something that you perceive to be negative, implies a persistent focus on the person, behavior or condition that you are tolerating, because once you no longer focus on it, you cease feeling a need to tolerate it.

For example, imagine that you are outside when a cold rain suddenly begins. Without an umbrella or rain coat, you wonder how long you will have to tolerate the discomfort of the rain until you can get to shelter. The longer it takes for you to get inside, the more frustrated you become and the more you notice yourself having to tolerate the discomfort. Your tolerance is not a solution to your discomfort; it is a reminder of it. Not until you get indoors does your frustration go away and you reach a point of acceptance with regard to the inclement weather. Take frustration away from tolerance, and you arrive at acceptance.

90.

Admission to college

"When I hear the word "tolerance" the impression it conveys to me is 'I don't like you, but I feel obligated to be nice to you and make you feel welcome because it's the right thing to do. I cannot stand certain things about you and feel that those things elevate me to a level superior to yours. But to keep the peace, I will put up with you.' "Acceptance" elicits a very different and far more positive response from me."

John Campbell, LLM
Lawyer and author

Imagine that you apply to two colleges for fall admission. The first college sends you a letter that states in part, *"We are pleased to inform you that we have decided to accept you for admission beginning in the fall."* From the second college you receive an apparently similar letter. It states in part, *"We are pleased to inform you that we have decided to tolerate your presence on campus, beginning in the fall."* All else being equal, which college would you rather attend? If tolerance really means acceptance, then those two letters should sound exactly the same to you. Do they?

IX.
Understanding

"Let us go beyond tolerance to build mutual understanding with respect, appreciation, and love for people whose religious traditions, symbols, and beliefs may differ from our own."

Unitarian Universalist Association's
1999 Statement of Conscience

"Inspired by the tragedy on September 11, 2001, the clergy at Temple Adat Elohim felt it necessary to reach beyond the word of tolerance and help the community at large achieve a better understanding and respect for other religions."

Temple Adat Elohim's series
"Beyond tolerance towards understanding"

The more we have in common, the easier it is to understand each other. Or is it that the more we understand each other, the more we realize we have in common? Probably both are true. In any event, understanding is an important component of any healthy relationship, constructive debate or peace process. We must ask then whether tolerance is a step down the path toward mutual understanding or does it form a barrier that discourages people from seeking to know one another. Answering that question will be the focus of this chapter.

91.
Tolerance protects prejudice

"Prejudice is the child of ignorance."
William Hazlitt
English author and philosopher

*"A person can be tolerant and prejudiced simultaneously. . . .
One can endure and refrain from acting intolerantly, but remain biased,
disapproving or judgemental. . . . We tend to assume that tolerance and
prejudice are opposites of each other, when in fact we can have both
simultaneously."*
From "Love Thy Neighbours"

Not only is it possible for tolerance and prejudice to co-exist, prejudice is a precursor for tolerance. When we judge others negatively and believe that we must endure their existence, tolerance is a natural reaction. An important part of the solution is to address the tendency to negatively prejudge people who are different from us, so that we can understand and even celebrate our differences.

92.

Understanding and tolerance are incompatible

"Let us not speak of tolerance. This negative word implies grudging concessions by smug consciences. Rather, let us speak of mutual understanding and mutual respect."

Father Dominique Pire
Belgian Dominican monk, Refugee advocate

"Classrooms in which acceptance of diversity rather than tolerance is evident are more student empowering . . . Introspection about prejudices will allow managers to move to understanding and acceptance and away from mere tolerance."

Stephanie Graham, Ed. D.
Associate Professor, Claremont Graduate School

If you truly understand someone, there is little need for tolerance. Conversely, as long as you think you need to tolerate someone, understanding seems unlikely and unnecessary. Suggesting that tolerance leads to understanding is like saying that holding your breath helps you to identify the scent in the air. Only by your willingness to inhale do you welcome the aroma into your experience. Understanding leads to acceptance, not tolerance.

93.

How does it feel to be ripped off?

"If men could only know each other,
they would neither idolize nor hate."

Elbert Hubbard
American author and philosopher

Imagine that you own a convenience store and are currently very tired and frustrated because you are stuck working at 2 AM; an employee didn't show up to relieve you when your last shift was over. Just then, while you are stocking shelves, someone comes into your store and steals several items. How do you feel? What would you do if you caught this person stealing from you? Would you press charges if the police identify and apprehend the criminal?

Now imagine another situation. A battered women runs out of her home in the middle of the night fearing that her abusive husband is about to kill her and her two-year old child. She had to leave so suddenly, that she didn't have time to find any money or her wallet and her child is hungry and crying. She comes into your store and not seeing anyone working there, takes a carton of milk and some bread for her hungry child and leaves you a note saying that she is running for her life and didn't have any money with her. How do you feel? What would you do if you caught this person leaving your store with the food? Would you press charges if the police identify and apprehend her? Is your answer to the questions the same for both situations? If not, why not?

They are actually the same situation. The only difference is that in the second situation, you had enough information to understand why the person took the food. In the first situation you might choose to tolerate what happened to you and not call the police. Or you might choose not to tolerate the theft and call the police or perhaps chase after the thief yourself. In the second situation, understanding seems more likely. And the more you understand why the person took the food, the less angry you are likely to be and the less you even consider tolerance to be an issue.

If tolerance becomes an issue at all, you are likely to wonder why this woman and her child have had to tolerate the abuse and you are probably glad that she decided to tolerate it no longer. You might imagine that if she chose to tolerate the abuse any longer, she and her child could have been seriously hurt or even killed. And you hope that her fleeing didn't place her in even greater danger.

In the first situation, the more you tolerate the thefts, the more angry you become. In the second situation, the more you understand the "thief" the less angry you become. Understanding and tolerance can thus have opposite effects on someone! Understanding can protect you from the need for tolerance. Unfortunately, tolerance can "protect" you from the possibility of understanding.

This example was not given to suggest that we should condone stealing. Instead, it suggests that instead of rushing to judgment, we should try to understand others. In this case, we come to learn that this was not an instance of simple theft. The woman wanted to pay for the items. Instead, this was an instance of a woman seeking to care for and protect her child and an opportunity for a store owner to provide humanitarian aid to them.

94.

Understanding or tolerating the broken furnace

Fighting hatred with tolerance is like "fixing" a broken furnace in your house by putting on more clothing. Such a solution helps you to "tolerate" the cold temperature without addressing the underlying problem. If you put enough clothes on, you might not have to deal with the broken furnace, because you shielded yourself from the cold. If you do not have enough clothing, your tolerance wears thin, and your frustration toward the furnace increases.

As an alternative, what if you do not seek a tolerance strategy and instead try to solve the problem by understanding its cause? You might discover that the furnace was not plugged in, that the furnace was not turned on, or that the furnace was working fine, but that you left many windows open in the house. Maybe you forgot to pay a fuel bill or perhaps you just do not know how to operate the furnace correctly.

Your willingness to understand the furnace could lead you to many possibilities and perhaps the best solution. It also invites you to consider whether it is you who needs to do something different rather than blame someone or something else. Tolerance on the other hand, distracts you from understanding by removing the symptom (e.g., feeling cold) and postpones a real solution. Tolerance limits our creativity while perpetuating our tendency to blame others when we are unhappy.

95.
A crying child

You have a young child who wakes up in the middle of the night, crying. You have at least three choices. First, you can tolerate the loud crying, perhaps by turning up the television to drown out the noise, by putting in ear plugs, or by moving to another part of the house so that you can't hear it (bad ideas). Second, you could choose not to tolerate it and go into the room and yell at the child and demand that the incessant crying comes to an end (another bad idea). Third, you could attempt to understand the crying (i.e., what it is that the child needs) so that you can solve the child's problem (e.g., change the diaper, offer some milk, provide other comfort, etc.) thereby making the crying unnecessary.

We would not suggest either of the first two options (i.e., tolerance or intolerance) only in part because of the concerns that child protective services would have with those approaches. Obviously, we would advise the third option because it is the only one that addresses both the child's and the parent's needs. It is difficult to imagine a situation in which tolerance is preferable to understanding.

Exercise 25: Vicious cycles

Purpose: To practice breaking out of destructive patterns by shifting our focus from what the other person is doing wrong to what we can do right.

Imagine you are in an argument with your friend and you are tired of what seems to be incessant criticism. The more she criticizes, the more you want to pull away or tune her out. The more you withdraw, however, the more she pursues you. And of course, the more she pursues, the more you feel a need to withdraw. The two of you are stuck in a vicious cycle. Your solution (backing away) is her problem, just as her solution (chasing after you) is your problem. Every time one of you attempts to solve your own problem, you make the other person's problem worse.

What is the solution? (Hint: It does not involve demanding, or waiting for, your friend to change. It also does not involve arguing about whose fault the argument is. The answer, however, will help you to see how seeking to understand someone is preferable to relying on tolerance if your goal is to resolve conflicts or strengthen relationships.)

96.
Marital bliss?

"Tolerance is not a basis for healthy human relationship nor will it ever lead to true community, for tolerance does not allow for learning, or growth or transformation, but rather ultimately keeps people in a state of suspended ignorance and conflict."

Victor Kazanjian

You work for Hallmark Cards in the "Romantic Card" division. During a focus group, participants talk about their relationships in an attempt to generate statements that you can use on your next batch of anniversary cards. You hear the following two statements about the basis of the love they feel for their spouse.

"The more I come to know and understand you, the more I love you."
"The more I learn how to tolerate you, the more I love you."

Which statement would you be more likely to include in a romantic card? Structurally, the two sentences are similar. But do they convey the same or similar message? Does the second sentence even make sense? Understanding and love fit so well together that it is easy to see how one leads to the other. In contrast, tolerance and love are antithetical, one inconsistent with the other, perhaps even preventing the other.

Support for this assertion can be found in some recent social science literature. John Gottman, Ph.D., a relationship expert, conducted a groundbreaking study in the 1990s examining the causes of divorce. Perhaps the most significant finding was that couples broke up not because of *what* they argued about (e.g., finances, sex, children, in-laws, etc.) but *how* they argued (e.g., how much criticism, contempt, defensiveness and stonewalling one or both used during arguments). The more they engaged in these behaviors, the less likely they would remain together or have a healthy relationship. For example, every time one partner criticized the other (as opposed to having merely complained about a problem) the relationship took a hit.

The bad news is that we all do some of these from time to time. The good news is that they are all choices, so we can work at no longer doing them. How does this fit into our discussion about tolerance? We have already identified the negative, judgmental, or critical attitude inherent in tolerance. So if criticism is a predictor of relationship deterioration or destruction and tolerance is rooted in that negative attitude, then what impact would you expect tolerance to have on personal, business or other relationships?

97.

The cost of not understanding

In January of 2007, a world-class musician was brought to Washington, D.C. to perform a concert. He brought with him his $3.5 million violin for his solo performance. He played beautifully several intricate Bach pieces for the 1097 people in attendance. His performance lasted almost an hour. Unlike his performance in Boston two nights earlier, at which each seat cost $100, this one was based entirely on voluntary donations – people paid whatever they thought it was worth to them.

Several remarkable things happened. First, nearly everyone walked out on this tremendous performance before it was over. Second, no one applauded in-between pieces or at the end. And third, he collected only $32 total (from 1097 people) for his effort, not even a third of what a single person who attended his Boston performance paid. How could this be? The answer is simple. His performance was underground at a metro station. The performance was arranged as a social science experiment by the Washington Post to see how people's perceptions would be affected by context.

One way to interpret the results is to consider the prejudgments people likely made of this man based on where he was playing. They did not expect him to be a world-class musician. More likely they expected him to be a struggling musician who at once was practicing his craft and panhandling to help pay the rent. Their expectations prevented them from appreciating what this man had to offer. This is also what happens when we harbor preconceived notions about members of various racial, religious, gender or other cultural groups. Our negative beliefs cause us to fear people who pose no real threat (e.g., one of the effects of racial profiling), and distract us from noticing all the valuable gifts each of us possess simply because we are part of the rich and diverse human community.

This story about the musician also serves as a reminder of the importance of setting aside time to listen to and understand the people in our lives. The commuters who were rushing through the metro station, probably had not put room in their schedule to enjoy a musical performance on their way to work. Consequently, they literally passed by a unique experience. What opportunities have the rest of us missed by not taking the time to understand and appreciate other people's experience?

98.

Can understanding cure tolerance?

"Tolerance does not require people to know anything at all about one another. As a result, tolerance can let us harbor all the stereotypes and half-truths that we want to believe about our neighbors. Tolerance does little to remove our ignorance of one another."

Diana L. Eck, Ph.D.
Professor of Comparative Religion and Indian Studies & Director of the Pluralism Project
Harvard University

How well do you have to understand someone to tolerate them? Not at all. The better you understand someone, the less likely you will feel a need to tolerate them. Try the following exercise on developing empathy.

Exercise 26: Heads or tails?

Purpose: To learn and practice an important empathy and compassion skill.

Someone flips a coin and asks you to call it. If you say either "heads" or "tails" you are speaking about your own limited perspective. Only if you say "both" are you speaking the truth about the coin.

What does the above statement mean, especially in terms of empathy and compassion? How can the result of a coin flip be both heads and tails? Does seeing only one side at a time mean that one side of the coin is more valid or real than the other side? If we held the coin up to a mirror we could see both sides at the same time. Even if we did that, however, how would our view of the backside of the coin differ from the one seen by the mirror? What does this exercise teach us about our ability to notice, understand and accept someone else's viewpoint that appears to contradict our own? If we increase our ability to "put ourselves into other people's shoes," what effect does this have on our perceived need to tolerate them? How many arguments, conflicts, even wars could be avoided or resolved if we came to realize that opposing views can both be right, legitimate or valid?

99.

Tolerance lacks courage

*"Courage is what it takes to stand up and speak;
courage is also what it takes to sit down and listen."*
Sir Winston Churchill
British Prime Minister and Nobel Laureate

The difference between tolerance and understanding is the difference between fear and courage. We need to find the courage to listen to people who are different from us. We also need to find the courage to listen to the voices of oppressed people who are telling us that they are offended by our tolerance of them. Consider this small sampling of what they have told me.

*"Who's this [tolerance] for anyway, the tolerator or the group of people
being tolerated? It's like you're patting yourself on the back for being
so generous as to put up with people you secretly despise."*
"Is that the best we can do? How pathetic!"
*"I always knew there was something wrong with it [tolerance];
I just couldn't put my finger on it."*
"Tolerance doesn't solve anything."
"Why would anyone want tolerance from another?"
*"That's the only bad word on your list [a list containing: acceptance,
appreciation, respect, tolerance, trust, and understanding]."*
"A wolf in sheep's clothing."
*"President [George W.] Bush claimed that the Republican Party is the
Party of Tolerance – as if that were a good thing."*
*"It's a trojan horse – dressed up as a gift, until you drop your guard
and let it inside. Then it doesn't feel so good."*
"Would you want to be tolerated?"
Study participants

X.

Appreciation and respect

"The new tolerance preserves symbols of disapproval, but it is embarrassed to act on them."

Dale Carpenter

"But isn't there something more than tolerance that I and we Freemasons should strive for? Shouldn't we always be striving to do even better than just "put up with" something we don't like? Tolerance means that I think that you are wrong and I am just forbearing your existence. Is it not a disrespect and irreverence to think that we are allowing others to live?"

Terry O. Trowbridge
Founder, Center for Reduction of Religious-Based Conflict

Consider the following statements found in diversity programs: *"Cultivating respect, appreciation and tolerance in the school." "Reduce student prejudice and promote positive attitudes toward tolerance, respect, and cultural appreciation." "Religious tolerance celebrates the inherent worth and dignity of all people . . . It fosters respect and appreciation of the differences between us."* The grouping of tolerance with appreciation and respect implies a consistency of message. Similarly, you might talk of valuing "peace, love and harmony" but would be unlikely to express interest in promoting "peace, love and disgust."

This leads to the question that we need to address in this chapter: *"Is tolerance consistent, or in conflict with, respect and appreciation?"* If we feel respected and appreciated when we discover someone's willingness to tolerate us, then we should consider including tolerance in our promotional campaigns. However, if tolerance leaves us feeling disrespected and unappreciated, we would do better to purge it from our thoughts and programs.

100.

Everyone on earth is a treasure

"Christian existence is not a matter of tolerance, but of love. The tolerant are superior to those they tolerate, as are the intolerant to those to whom they object; it is not so with love."

Rev. Craig Thompson

Consider the following assertion: *"Tolerance fundamentally is a decision . . . a belief that every other person on earth is a treasure"* (from a website extolling the virtues of tolerance). Rather than blindly accept that statement as true, we decided to test it in our study. We included the following item *"John treasures his relationship with Bill."* If it is true that tolerance is a way of treasuring others, then tolerance should have been endorsed at least as often as the other concepts (i.e., respect, appreciation, understanding, acceptance, and trust).

We found, however, just the opposite to be true. Respondents felt that appreciation (56%) most reflected viewing others as treasures, followed next by respect (32%). In contrast, not even a single respondent believed that tolerance was the best fit. This makes sense. Imagine someone trying to reassure his spouse, *"How can you doubt how much I treasure our life together? After all, I've tolerated you for over 20 years."*

Be prepared for a night on the couch!

101.

Tolerance lacks dignity

"Where is the dignity in being told that your beliefs and very existence will be tolerated?"
"Tolerance feels like quiet humiliation."
Study participants

"The quality or state of being worthy of esteem or respect"
Dictionary definition of "dignity"

According to Robert W. Fuller, author of several books (e.g., "All rise: Somebodies, nobodies and the politics of dignity," Berrett-Koehler, 2006), power and rank are not problems per se. The problem is the abuse of power and using higher rank to humiliate and exploit subordinates. He coined the term "rankism" to refer to that abuse of rank. He promotes forming a "dignitarian society" in which the inherent worth of everyone is acknowledged, regardless of their rank or status.

Exercise 27: Creating a dignitarian society

Purpose: To examine the relationship between tolerance and dignity as a way of determining whether being tolerant is a respectful way of interacting with others.

How does tolerance support or interfere with the development of a dignitarian society? Do you feel respected by those who are willing to tolerate you or do you feel "quietly" humiliated as one of the study participants quoted above does? Think of a time when you felt that someone treated you with dignity. Did you attribute that experience to the other person's willingness to be tolerant? If you were hired to be the architect of a dignitarian society, what conceptual tools would you include in your tool box? Would they include respect, acceptance or other concepts?

102.

Value to society

"Tolerance is a very dull virtue. It is boring. Unlike love, it has always had a bad press. It is negative. It merely means putting up with people, being able to stand things."

E.M. Forster
English novelist

Another way to assess whether tolerance reflects viewing others as treasures is to ask about their contribution to society. In response to *"John thinks Bill has a lot to offer to society,"* respondents thought John was most likely to respect Bill (59%). Twenty five percent thought John appreciated Bill. Tolerance was the only concept that received no endorsements at all. Once you find yourself tolerating someone, you are not focusing on anything positive that they have to offer. You are only concerned with some perceived flaw(s) that you are being asked to endure.

Still not convinced that tolerance is an inadequate substitute for appreciation? Try this. Imagine that you and a coworker are retiring at the same time after 25 years of dedicated service. At your joint retirement party, the CEO turns first to your colleague and states, *"This plaque can only begin to demonstrate how much we have appreciated your being part of this company."*

He then grabs another plaque, turns to you and says *"This plaque can only begin to show you how much we have tolerated your being part of this company."* How appreciated would you feel while receiving this gift of tolerance in front of all your co-workers, family and friends?

103.

Think green

"I said 'celebrate,' not 'tolerate.' In our complex and hurting world, putting up with the differences between us is not enough. We need to continue to stretch our boundaries and recognize that truth for one is not necessarily truth for all."

John Brierly McCall, D. Min.

While I was researching this book, I wondered what advice an environmentalist would have for addressing hatred and discrimination. It made me think about when I was growing up. Throughout the week, my family would throw everything we didn't want into a garbage bag and then cart it off to the dump. Not very environmentally friendly but we weren't thinking along those lines. To us it was only garbage, so we got rid of it. It was a type of ecological segregation.

Today we drive to a recycling center. Inside the facility there are separate bins for cans, glass, plastic, cardboard, newspapers, etc. After we distribute these reusable resources, there is far less garbage for our community to tolerate. The garbage hasn't changed since I was growing up, only our ability to see it differently, to identify resources where once we saw nothing of value.

Perhaps our thinking can evolve in a similar way with regards to people who are different from us. Too often, all we see is someone who is foreign, a threat, or an enemy rather than a neighbor, a resource or a friend. We need to learn how to see the inherent worth in others, especially those who make us most uncomfortable. To illustrate, I'll give you an example from my own experience.

When I was in college, there was an annoying man in our dorm. It seemed that a day didn't go by without him finding fault in what someone said, did, wore, etc. We did our best to tolerate him, assuming that that was just part of college life. One day, though, I noticed my tolerance wearing thin (as it inevitably does) and was tempted to lash out by giving him a piece of my mind. Instead, I decided to try an experiment. I had an English paper due in a few days and asked him if he would be willing to edit it for me. It stood to reason that someone who invested so much energy detecting other people's faults would have the requisite skills to detect grammatical and other kinds of errors in my paper. Sure enough, he eagerly accepted my invitation and did an excellent job editing my paper. What's more, I quickly fell off his list of people to criticize and we actually became pretty good friends.

What I learned is that sometimes what appears to be someone else's negative trait, is actually a valuable skill, negatively applied or perceived. By challenging myself to detect resources where previously I saw only flaws, I was able to avoid confrontation and strengthen a relationship. I also noticed that the resentment that had built up due to feeling that I had to tolerate his obnoxiousness, just disappeared, leading me to feel better about both him and myself.

Exercise 28: Converting flaws into strengths

Purpose: To discover how changing our perceptions can improve our relationships by reducing frustration, fear, anger and conflict.

Think about a person or group of people who bother you. Identify what it is about them that most irritates or repulses you (for me it was my neighbor's incessant criticism). Now ask yourself what skill or strength can be found in that trait or behavior. How could that skill, if applied differently, benefit you or someone else? Is there a way for you to help them channel that skill in a productive manner? What would be your first step? How would your life change if you were successful in helping them to convert that apparent flaw into a resource? How might other people's lives change? What would happen if we routinely asked ourselves these questions each time we found ourselves disapproving of others?

104.
What a pain!

My ninth grade English teacher told me that "*'Nice' is what you call someone when you have nothing nice to say about them.*" Similarly, to say that you tolerate someone, is faint praise at best. But is it worse than that? Does it merely convey lukewarm admiration or does it actually contradict appreciation? To help answer that, consider the responses to the following items in our survey:

"*John finds it painful to be around Bill*" (Tolerance 86%; Acceptance 7%; Understanding 4%)

"*John did not like it one bit when Bill moved into the neighborhood*" (Tolerance 86%; Understanding 7%; Acceptance 5%)

"*John wishes Bill would just go away*" (Tolerance 86%; Understanding 7%; Appreciation and Respect 3% each; Acceptance 2%).

Is tolerance the "nicest" gift we can offer someone we have not learned to appreciate very much?

105.

"Close the book on hate"

"To simply be tolerant doesn't feel too good. People should have a deep sense of appreciation of people different from them."

David Odell-Scott
Associate Professor of Philosophy, Kent State University

The Anti-Defamation League in partnership with Barnes and Noble produced an extensive guide for addressing hatred. The last page of the guide is a campaign pledge that asks the undersigned to interrupt prejudice, become aware of our own biases and to stop others who, because of hatred, would violate the civil rights of others. The pledge extols the virtues of respect, understanding individual and group differences, and equality. But nowhere does the pledge ask us to be more tolerant. "Close the Book on Hate" lists over 100 strategies for fighting hate. While it does identify intolerance as part of the problem, nowhere does it suggest that tolerance should be part of the solution.

106.
Walking on hot coals

Why would anyone want to stroll barefoot across a path of charcoal briquettes, glowing orange with heat? The answer for some is that it allows them to test their limits and challenge some of their most basic assumptions (e.g., *"If I step on something that is burning at a thousand degrees, I will suffer painful injury"*).

It was a cold January evening in NYC when about 30 of us gathered in a school classroom to learn about fire walking. While one of the instructors was outside, within view, stoking the fire, we were inside listening to the other instructor facilitate a conversation about fears and limiting beliefs.

"In about an hour, we will take off our shoes, go outside and form a circle around the burning embers to prepare for our walk. But before we do, I need you to consider two very important questions. First, what is the worst thing you can imagine happening to you as a result of walking across the hot coals?" I imagined burning flesh and severe pain followed by a stint in the hospital attempting to heal with the aid of skin grafts. *"Now I want you to ask yourself if you could accept that outcome. Not if you want that outcome, or would enjoy it. Merely, could you survive it? Because if your answer is "no" then you should not attempt to walk across the coals. Only if your answer is "yes" will you be able to free yourself from imagining the worst and open yourself to the possibility of the best – a wonderful, pain-free and possibly life-changing experience."*

All thirty of us decided we could survive it and out the door we went. The result: Everyone walked across the coals (at least twice!) with only one person suffering any blisters. And even for that person, the blisters were no worse than what would be acquired from wearing a new pair of tight shoes.

The first time I walked across, it felt like I was walking through snow – hardly what I had anticipated. The second time, my feet felt warm, but by no means uncomfortable. Afterwards, as we were sharing our experiences with each other, the most common reaction was along the lines of *"I never thought I could do this. I wonder what other negative beliefs I have that have been limiting my life."* One message became clear to me. If we prejudge a person or situation as negative (as we do when we talk about needing to tolerate a group or class of people), the result likely would be a self-fulfilling prophecy. If, however, we put aside our expectations, fears and labels and instead seek to understand people for who they really are, a vibrant world opens up for us, one that is not marred by prejudice, hatred, violence and war.

Exercise 29: Limiting beliefs

Purpose: To increase awareness of the effect of limiting beliefs on our relationships, personal safety and happiness.

Think of a deeply held limiting belief you have about others (e.g., "All women are unreasonable," "All men are insensitive," "People from a particular religion, race or culture can never be trusted," or "My spouse will never understand me.") These beliefs often come in the form of all-or-nothing statements. Now imagine what would happen if you suspended that belief, searched for an exception to what you believe that rule to be. Generalizations are never true (irony intended). How might your life or relationships improve if you let go of the beliefs that are holding you back, putting barriers between you and others? How many friends and allies could you find amongst those who currently seem to you to be threatening or even your enemies?

107.
Respect and tolerance are incompatible

"My memory had taught me that my humanity is defined by yours. Even when my faith is different from yours, it is neither superior nor inferior in its authenticity. Is its name tolerance? No: tolerance could suggest condescendence, and I prefer the word 'respect'."

Elie Wiesel
Nobel Laureate and Holocaust survivor

"It [tolerance] feels so disrespectful."
"If you treat people with respect, why would you need tolerance?"

Study participants

You cannot promote both respect and tolerance. If you respect someone, you look up to them. If you tolerate them, you look down at them. One person's eyes cannot do both simultaneously.

108.
Corporal punishment

"I'm not going to tolerate any more acting out from you!"
"It's my job to teach my son respect!"
A frustrated father

I find it both interesting and discouraging that the U.S. and many other countries still condone the hitting of children. If someone did exactly the same behavior to an adult, the perpetrator would be convicted of a violent crime. I used to believe the "educational" excuse that it was a parent's responsibility to teach or discipline their children. But then I noticed that fewer and fewer jurisdictions allow teachers to hit children even though they also are responsible for teaching and disciplining those children. The difference is that parents are viewed as owning their children, whereas teachers do not own their students. The issue therefore is not education, but property rights. *"No one is going to hit my child!"* is what parents might say while they are seeking to have a teacher fired for spanking their child. And yet they might not rule out their own use of spanking if that child misbehaves in the same way at home.

What if we took a different approach? What if we thought that children deserved equal protection under the law? What if we truly believed that they deserved to be safe from violence, even violence perpetrated by their parents? What if instead of asking ourselves whether we should tolerate a child's misbehavior, we instead insisted on understanding their behavior and respectfully guiding them toward better decisions? Perhaps then we could avoid teaching them that when you disapprove of someone's behavior it is OK to beat that person into compliance. Perhaps they would respect us as parents, not because they have to, but because we earned it through our own respectful actions. Do unto others, . . .

"If we really want a peaceful and compassionate world, we need to build communities of trust where all children are respected, where home and school are safe places to be and where discipline is taught by example."
Desmond M. Tutu
Archbishop Emeritus, Global initiative to End All
Corporal Punishment of Children, 2006

109.

Deciding whether someone is a threat or a resource

"I have begun to understand tolerance as being a major barrier to attaining a healthy, just, peaceful human community."

Victor Kazanjian

Consider this example shared with me by a child protective social worker. Upon arrival at a family's house, the CPS workers informed the father that they were responding to a call of suspected abuse and neglect. As it turns out, there was no abuse or neglect. The workers were sent to the wrong house. Now imagine how you would feel if you thought you were being accused of hurting your own children, especially by some government agency that under certain circumstances is granted the authority to take custody of those children! How would you respond? You understandably might be outraged. Would you want to slam the door in their faces? Demand to know who would file such a report against you or insist on speaking to your attorney before allowing them to set foot in your house? While these are perfectly understandable and common reactions, they are not how this father responded.

First, he thanked the workers for coming by. Next, he invited them to come in to meet his wife and children. Finally, he asked them if they wouldn't mind telling him more about what a CPS agency does since he had never been involved with them. (Before reading further, see if you can think of why he stayed so calm and why he was so welcoming of people falsely accusing him of being an unfit parent at best. Even the workers were surprised at his reaction.)

As he explained it to them, he was glad to see that there were other people who cared about his children as much as he did. *"It's good to know that if my children were in danger or if I were struggling as a parent, that someone would be there to offer support."* As he later explained, *"Since I had done nothing wrong, there was no reason for me to be defensive. Besides, being defensive makes me look guilty, only making matters worse. And if I had fallen short as a parent, I could probably benefit from their services. Either way, working with them would always be preferable to guarding against them.*" Before they left, they described various services and supports that were available to parents.

Within the next year, he was laid off causing significant financial stress. Fortunately, he remembered a few assistance programs the CPS worker had described to him and called to sign up for temporary help. He also attended a support group for parents, which he said *"made all the difference in the world."* By being open to viewing CPS as a valuable resource rather than a threat to his family, he was better able to provide for and protect his loved ones. *People are not problems. They are resources to help solve problems.*

110.

Where do we go from here?

> **Even the worst criminal at one time acted with compassion. Even the person with the highest character at one time said or did something that was hurtful.**

In deciding what to do about tolerance, let us not make the mistake of taking sides. There is room for everyone at this table. We need everyone. Let us not forget that people are not the problem, people are resources to help solve problems. Violence, abuse, terrorism, hatred and discrimination are problems. Hunger, natural disasters, climate change and disease are problems. We cannot afford to be at war with each other when there are so many other problems that require our collaborative efforts. For too long we have resembled a snake intent on swallowing its own tail.

*If you or your organization has promoted tolerance, you are a pioneer, someone who has helped us to shine a light on a difficult concept. We will need your insights and experience as we move beyond tolerance to a less judgmental and safer world.

*If you have been a target of oppression, we need your participation. Only you know what it is like for you to be looked down upon, to be ostracized or marginalized. Until now, we have not asked you how you felt about tolerance. As one of our study participants said, *"I always knew that there was something wrong with tolerance, but who was I to speak up? I didn't want to appear ungrateful."* Another said, *"These are great organizations. I just assumed it was my fault that I was offended by their tolerance campaign."* I regret that we have silenced you in this way. Your voice needs to be heard. It is time for us to listen and take you seriously.

*If you harbor hate, we need you as well. We need to know what it is that you fear. Why do people who are different from you feel so threatening? What is it like when we ask you to be more tolerant? Does it help or does it just make you feel even more resentful?

*Finally, if you already are concerned about the promotion of tolerance, we need you to speak up, spread the word, and express your concerns. *Change one word, change the world.* We need you to continue to challenge any word, idea, concept or ideology that suggests that one group of people is better than or more deserving than another. We can all be different without being better or worse. Reassure others that being equal does not mean that they have to be identical or agree with everything someone else does or believes. As a bumper sticker I saw recently said: *"God is too big to fit into any one religion."* There is room for us all on the same level playing field.

Exercise 30: Cost-benefit analysis

Purpose: To use a simple checklist of questions to evaluate what role if any we think tolerance should play in our efforts to achieve equality.

Once everyone is around the table, how do we decide whether to abandon tolerance or any other concept that causes us concern? You can decide for yourself by performing a simple cost-benefit analysis. To do this, consider benefits, risks and alternatives. Do the benefits outweigh the risks and is the option you are considering (e.g., promoting tolerance) the best of all available alternatives?

For example, if we go back to the section on the problem of giving aspirin to children, we realize that:

(a) the benefit of aspirin is that it reduces pain and/or fever;

(b) the risk is the possibility of the child developing life-threatening Reyes Syndrome; but fortunately,

(c) even though the risks outweigh the benefits, there are ample alternatives such as ibuprofen which can assist with pain and fever but do not increase the risk of developing Reyes. Consequently, our cost-benefit analysis tells us that aspirin for children is not worth the risk.

We need to perform the same type of analysis with the promotion of potentially problematic concepts such as tolerance.

Benefits: Do you think that there is a clear benefit to promoting tolerance? The people in our study could not report any. However, many well-respected individuals and organizations think there are. Ask people who are tolerant or who promote tolerance what they see as the advantages. Ask those who are being tolerated what, if anything, they like most about the concept.

Risks: Do you think that promoting tolerance can cause any problems? People in our study and many civic and religious leaders reported multiple concerns such as believing that tolerance conveyed a condescending attitude, was insulting, led to confusion and resentment and reinforced the power imbalance between the person being tolerant and the one being tolerated.

Alternatives: Is tolerance necessary? Are we unable to fight hatred and discrimination without it? Is there something positive that tolerance offers that other concepts do not? Would something be missing if we left it out? I have yet to hear any unique benefits of tolerance that were not offered by other terms such as acceptance, respect, understanding, equality, appreciation, embracing diversity, inclusiveness, and openness. Can you think of any unique benefits of tolerance?

What was written in these pages was not intended to serve as the final word on tolerance. Instead, it was intended to be the beginning of a long-overdue conversation about a very large elephant in the living room. Tolerance, though, is not the first pachyderm to visit us. The "separate-but-equal" variety sat with us virtually unnoticed for over half a century. Let us not allow history to repeat itself. Welcome to the conversation.

Sources

A common word. "A common word between us and you." Retrieved December 12, 2008 from website: www.acommonword.com.

Alliance Defense Fund. "The Defense of Marriage Act watch." Retrieved January 12, 2010 from website: http://www.domawatch.org/index.php.

Anti-defamation League (2001). "Close the book on hate." Retrieved January 5, 2007 from website: http://www.adl.org/Prejudice/default.asp.

The Better World Project. Retrieved December 16, 2009 from website: www.betterworld.net/quotes.

Bodendorfer, G. (1997). "Beyond tolerance: Christian-Jewish dialogue in the next millennium." *Jewish Christian Relations.* Retrieved November 11, 2009 from website: www.jcrelations.net/en/?itemm=803.

Brainy Quote. Retrieved January 04, 2010 from website: www.brainyquote.com.

Campbell, J. H. (2002). "Beyond tolerance." Retrieved December 12, 2009 from website: www.whosoever.org/v616/campbell.html.

Capenter, D. (2000). "The new tolerance." Retrieved January 09, 2010 from website: www.outsmartmagazine.com/issue/i09-00/outright.html.

Center for Reduction of Religious-Based Conflict. Retrieved January 05, 2010 from website: www.center2000.org.

Chemerinsky, E. Lawrence v. Texas. Retrieved January 11, 2010 from website: www.law.duke.edu/publiclaw/supremecourtonline/commentary/lawvtex.

Civil Rights Project at UCLA. Retrieved January 04, 2010 from website: http://www.civilrightsproject.ucla.edu/research/metro/three_metros.php.

Coen, F. E. (2002). "Beyond tolerance, pluralism." Retrieved January 02, 2010 from website: http://www.confronti.net/oldconfronti/english/archives/jan02.htm.

Convention on the elimination of all forms of discrimination against women. Retrieved December 10, 2009 from website: www.un.org/womenwatch/daw/cedaw/reports.htm.

Cromer, C. A Taoist perspective. Retrieved November 12, 2006 from website: http://reocities.com/Athens/aegean/7201/ taoistcircle.html.

Dictionary.com. Retrieved January 10, 2010 from website: www. dictionary.com.

Eck, Diana. The Pluralism Project. Retrieved December 15, 2006 from website: http://pluralism.org/pluralism/essays/from_ diversity_to_pluralism.php.

Education World. Retrieved December 16, 2007 from website: www.educationworld.com.

Freyd, J. & Johnson, J.Q. (1998). "Commentary: Domestic violence, folk etymologies, & 'Rule of Thumb'." Retrieved December 22, 2009 from website: http://dynamic.uoregon.edu/~jjf/essays/ruleofthumb.html.

Gandhi, A. (2003) "Legacy of love: My education in the path of non-violence." North Bay Books, El Sobrante, CA, page 127.

Gossett Jr. L. The Eracism Foundation. Retrieved October 10, 2009 from website: www.ereacismfoundation.org.

Gottman, J. M. & Silver, N. (2000). The seven principles for making marriage work. Crown Publishing, NY, NY.

Graham, Stephanie, (1998). "Diversity . . . report card: Lessons from the creators of our work force." *Training for the Los Angeles County Office of Education*, LA, CA.

Hampton, S. (2004). Rethinking tolerance. Retrieved January 15, 2010 from website: www.endingtheviolence.us.

Kiernan, L. A. (posted June 5, 1993). "Victim stunned by NH judge's comments, sentence in domestic assault prompts outrage." Boston Globe. Retrieved December 15, 2009 from website: http://www.encyclopedia.com/doc/1P2-8230704.html.

Kubler-Ross, E. (1969). "On death and dying." Scribner, NY, NY.

Landmark Cases. Retrieved January 04, 2010 from website: www.landmarkcases.org/plessy/home.html.

Lincoln, A. "The Gettysburg address." Retrieved January 07, 2010 from website: http://americancivilwar.com/north/lincoln.html.

Lyrics Time. Retrieved January 07, 2010 from website: www.lyricstime.com.

McMahon, J. J. (2007). "Marital rape laws, 1976-2002: From exemptions to prohibitions" *Paper presented at the annual meeting of the American Sociological Association.* NY, NY. Retrieved September 15, 2009 from http://www.allacademic.com/meta/p183005_index.html.

Martin Luther King Online. Retrieved January 05, 2010 from website: www.mlkonline.net/dream.html.

McCall, John Brierly (1/11/2004). "Beyond tolerance." A sermon at First Congregational Church of the United Church of Christ, South Portland, Maine.

Merriam-Webster Dictionary. Retrieved January 03, 2010 from website: www.merriam-webster.com/dictionary/tolerance.

National Reye's Syndrome Foundation. Retrieved January 06, 2010 from website: www.reyessyndroome.org.

Neibuhr, R. "The serenity prayer" Retrieved January 10, 2010 from website: www.aahistory.com/prayer.html.

Neill, A.S. "Summerhill" Retrieved January 11, 2010 from website: http://www.scribd.com/doc/5081386/summerhill 8/26/2008.

Quote World. Retrieved December 22, 2010 from website: www.quoteworld.org.

Ontario Consultants on Religious Tolerance. Retrieved January 08, 2010 from website: www.religioustolerance.org.

Pence, E. & Paymar, M. (2000). Education groups for men who batter. Springer, NY, NY, page 96.

Persky, A. S. (posted October 01, 2008). "Don't ask, don't tell: Don't work? ABA Journal Online. Retrieved January 10, 2010 from website: www.abajournal.com/magazine/article/dont_ask_dont_tell_dont_work.

President's Task Force on Gay, Bisexual, Lesbian, and Transgender Issues (2001). "Affirming diversity: Moving from tolerance to acceptance and beyond." University of Washington. Retrieved January 06, 2010 from website: http://www.washington.edu/reports/gblt/gblt.pdf.

Prostitution Research and Education. Retrieved October 15, 2009 from website: www.prostitutionresearch.com/laws/000024.html.

Shaw, C. G. (2002). "Beyond tolerance." Retrieved October, 12, 2009 from website: www.newsreview.com.

Southern Poverty Law Center. Retrieved November 07, 2006 & January 05, 2010 from website: www.splcenter.org.

Temple Adat Elohim. "Beyond tolerance toward understanding" lecture series. Retrieved December 15, 2009 from website: www.thechurchoftheepiphany.org/Resources/The_Star_March_03.pdf.

The Golden Rule. Retrieved December 12, 2009 from website: www.thegoldenrule.net/quotes.htm.

The King Center. "Pledge of nonviolence in honor of Dr. Martin Luther King, Jr." Retrieved Dececmber 12, 2007 from website: http://www.thekingcenter.org/prog/non/pledge.pdf.

The Martin Luther King, Jr. Research and Education Institute. "King papers project" Retrieved from website: http://mlk-kpp01.stanford.edu.

Think Exist. Retrieved November 22, 2009 from website: www.thinkexist.com.

Thomas, T. & Witenberg, R. (2004). "Love thy neighgbours: Racial tolerance among young Australians." Retrieved January 05, 2010 from website: http://amf.net.au/library/file/Love_Thy_Neighbours_Report.pdf.

Thompson, Rev. Craig (2004). "Being church: Moving beyond tolerance." Retrieved May 15, 2008 from website: www.theyouinme.org/fall_2004.pdf.

Tutu, Desmond (2006). Retrieved January 03, 2010 from website: www.nospank.net/pt2009.htm.

Twain Quotes. Retrieved December 28, 2009 from website: www.twainquotes.com.

Unitarian Universalist Association. Retrieved October 23, 2009 from website: www.uua.org/visitors/6798.shtml.

UShistory.org. "The Declaration of Independence." Retrieved January 05, 2010 from website: www.ushistory.org/declaration.

Walker, Lenore (1980). "The battered woman." HarperCollins, NY, NY.

Weingarten, G. (posted 04/08/07) "Pearls before breakfast." The Washington Post.

Wiesel, E. (posted 06/11/2006). Dartmouth commencement speech. Retrieved November 08, 2010 from website: http://www.dartmouth.edu/~news/releases/2006/06/11a.html.

Wilkie, W. World of quotes. Retrieved December 15, 2009 from website: www.worldofquotes.com.

List of Authorities

LaVergne, TN USA
16 August 2010
193531LV00005B/5/P